Sharing the Word

Simple Theology
Theology for the rest of us

Clay A. Kahler

Wipf and Stock Publishers
150 West Broadway • Eugene OR 97401

Wipf and Stock Publishers
150 West Broadway
Eugene, Oregon 97401

Simple Theology: Theology for the Rest of Us
By Kahler, Clay A.
©2002 Kahler, Clay A.
ISBN: 1-57910-887-3
Publication Date: February, 2002

Special thanks to those who helped make this work possible:

Dr. Gary Coombs

Dr. George Hare

Dr. George Goolde

Dr. Garland Shin

Dr. Marvin Lubenow

Dr. Gary Woods

Pastor David Myers

Bruce Leary

All of the staff and faculty at Southern California Bible College & Seminary

The Members of Campo Baptist Church

Table of Contents

Foreword 9

Christology (The Doctrine of Christ) 11

Theology Proper (The Doctrine of God) 27

Pneumatology (The Doctrine of the Holy Spirit) 53

Soteriology (The Doctrine of Salvation) 65

Bibliology (The Doctrine of the Bible) 77

Eschatology (The Doctrine of End Times) 113

Hamartiology (The Doctrine of Sin) 125

Anthropology (The Doctrine of Man) 133

Angelology (The Doctrine of Spirit Beings) 143

Dispensationalism 157

    Appendix 171

    Selected Bibliography 177

    Subject Index 191

    Index of Persons 205

Foreword

In a day when few Christians seem to know what they believe, and when few Christians want to take the time to research the basic doctrines of their faith, this book is a timely tool for those wanting to get started with their personal research.

Just what do you believe about the Doctrine of the Bible, the Doctrine of the Triune God, the Doctrine of the Holy Spirit, etc.? Is what you believe about these doctrines of our Christian faith based on your intense search of the Scriptures, or have you just been content to inherit what you have heard through the years? We are living in a world where all the absolutes of God's truth are being challenged & denied. This same world is full of people looking for the answers to life. The Apostle Peter was looking at a similar world, a place where believers needed to separate themselves from the evils of the world, endure the sufferings in their lives, and declare the reasons for the hope that was within them (1 Peter 3:15).

You and I also need to share the hope that is within us. That sharing could be as simple as our personal testimony of how we accepted Christ as our Savior; however, it could also be the defense of our faith – what do we believe and why do we believe it. Are you ready for that kind of defense should you be asked?

Most folks are not motivated to start their research by reading a book on systematic theology. If you are one of those, might I suggest this book by Clay Kahler. This book is designed to present the basic doctrines of our faith in a non-technical, easy-reading style that will keep you interested until the end of the book. It is not the author's intention to cover every aspect of all the doctrines, but rather to touch on the main issues about those doctrines that you may encounter from those searching for answers. I read this book through on two separate occasions, each time without stopping. My gut feelings is that the reading of this book will motivate many to do additional research into their basic beliefs – yes, possibly to even read the systematic theology book.

Clay and I met at Southern California Bible College & Seminary as students, and we have taught Bible college courses together to prison inmates. I know that Clay's desire is to "accurately handle the Word of Truth" and to use his gifts to "equip the saints". I count it a privilege to stand with Clay in inviting you into the pages of this book.

Bruce Leary, Director
Southwest College of Biblical Studies
Pine Valley, California

Christology
(The Doctrine of Christ)

What are we to make of Jesus Christ? This is a question, which has, in a sense, a frantically comic side. For the real question is not what are we to make of Christ, but what is He to make of us. The picture of a fly sitting deciding what it is going to make of an elephant has comic elements about it.
 -C.S. Lewis in God in the Doc

Who is Jesus?
Who was this man for whom millions have died and for whom men are beaten and families have been torn apart. In this study I will show that Jesus was first the Christ, the Messiah. Then I will make an attempt to determine from the Scriptures that He

is God. And then I will touch on His redemptive work (*See Soteriology*).

Is Jesus the Messiah?
In His first promises of a Messiah or a redeemer, a savior for the children of Israel and even the world, God made many very specific prophecies. There were prophecies concerning His lineage, His birth, His life and death, His victory and His reign. These prophecies started out fairly broad. The Messiah would be of the seed of Eve, the first woman. Then it was prophesied that the Messiah would come from the children of Abraham, the tribe of Judah, the lineage of King David. Then the virgin birth was prophesied, the location of the birth and then even a time frame for events in His life. We will not look at all of the prophecies but we will look at each area.

The Lineage of the Messiah
The Messiah would come of the seed of a woman, the seed of Eve.

> And I will put enmity between you and the woman, and between your seed and her Seed; He shall bruise your head, and you shall bruise His heel."
>
> -Genesis 3:15

This is significant because the Hebrew word used here for seed is singular as in one person, not plural as in the nation Israel. It is also significant in that it alludes to the later prophesied virgin birth.

The Messiah would be of the children of Abraham.

> I will make you a great nation; I will bless you and make your name great; and you shall be a blessing. I will bless those who bless you, And

> I will curse him who curses you; And in you all the families of the earth shall be blessed."
>
> —Genesis 12:2-3

In Abraham all of the families of the earth will be blessed. The sins of the world would be atoned for through the children of Abraham through the son of Abraham.

The Messiah would be of the tribe of Judah

> The scepter shall not depart from Judah, Nor a lawgiver from between his feet, Until Shiloh comes; And to Him shall be the obedience of the people.
>
> -Genesis 49:10

The prophecies broaden from the nation to the tribe. Of all of the twelve tribes, it was prophesied that Judah would bring forth the promised one of God.

The Messiah would come from the seed of David the King

> "When your days are fulfilled and you rest with your fathers, I will set up your seed after you, who will come from your body, and I will establish his kingdom. He shall build a house for My name, and I will establish the throne of his kingdom forever. I will be his Father, and he shall be My son. If he commits iniquity, I will chasten him with the rod of men and with the blows of the sons of men. But My mercy shall not depart from him, as I took it from Saul, whom I removed from before you. And your house and your kingdom shall be established forever before you. Your throne shall be established forever."
>
> -2 Samuel 7:12-16

David, the King of Israel, the one who was called the "apple of God's eye" would be the direct ancestor of the Messiah. This was not the only revelation concerning this passage, not only would the Messiah be of David's lineage, but the Messiah would rule on David's throne forever.

The Birth of the Messiah

The Manner of the Messiah's Birth
> Therefore the Lord Himself will give you a sign: Behold, the virgin shall conceive and bear a Son, and shall call His name Immanuel.
> -Isaiah 7:14

This may be one of the boldest prophecies of the Messiah. He would be born of a virgin. This supernatural act would be the stage upon which He the Messiah would arrive. This links directly with the prophecy from Genesis 3:15 which stated that He would be of "her seed."

The Place of the Messiah's Birth
> "But you, Bethlehem Ephrathah, Though you are little among the thousands of Judah, yet out of you shall come forth to Me the One to be Ruler in Israel, whose goings forth are from of old, from everlasting."
> -Micah 5:2

Any self-respecting Jew would have wagered his whole birthright on the fact that the Messiah of God would have no doubt been born in the Holy of Holies in the Temple of Jerusalem. Instead they received the prophecy that the Blessed One would be born in the small insignificant town of His father David.

The Life of the Messiah

The Messenger of the Messiah

> The voice of one crying in the wilderness: "Prepare the way of the LORD; Make straight in the desert A highway for our God. Every valley shall be exalted And every mountain and hill brought low; The crooked places shall be made straight And the rough places smooth; The glory of the LORD shall be revealed, And all flesh shall see it together; For the mouth of the LORD has spoken."
>
> -Isaiah 40:3-5

Yet another clue was given to the people of Israel. A messenger would precede the Messiah. One crying in the wilderness who would call for repentance and proclaim the coming of the Messiah. A messenger who would prepare the way for God's chosen One.

The Mission of the Messiah

> The Spirit of the Lord GOD is upon Me, because the LORD has anointed Me to preach good tidings to the poor; He has sent Me to heal the brokenhearted, to proclaim liberty to the captives, and the opening of the prison to those who are bound;
>
> - Isaiah 61:1

The Messiah would be a man on a mission, a man who would work against the normal status quo. He would be sent to the undesirables and the unloved ones. He would preach good news to the poor. He would heal the broken hearts of those who were sorrowful and dejected. He would proclaim liberty to those in bondage and he would set those free who were oppressed.

The Ministry of the Messiah
> Surely He has borne our griefs and carried our sorrows; yet we esteemed Him stricken, smitten by God, and afflicted. But He was wounded for our transgressions, He was bruised for our iniquities; the chastisement for our peace was upon Him, and by His stripes we are healed. All we like sheep have gone astray; we have turned, every one, to his own way; and the LORD has laid on Him the iniquity of us all.
>
> -Isaiah 53:4

The Messiah would be a man of ministry. He would bear the sins of the world. He would reestablish that broken fellowship that we once had with the Father. The Messiah would be a man who through His own suffering would provide us peace with God.

The Message of the Messiah
> I will open my mouth in a parable; I will utter dark sayings of old,
>
> -Psalm 78:2

The Messiah would be a man with a message. He would arrive on the scene and He would teach the deep things of God, with an authority and a skill that is unmatched. He would use the art of story telling to accomplish this and He would exercise power in his message.

The March of the Messiah
> Rejoice greatly, O daughter of Zion! Shout, O daughter of Jerusalem! Behold, your King is coming to you; He is just and having salvation, lowly and riding on a donkey, a colt, the foal of a donkey.
>
> -Zechariah 9:9

So many times in the past the great kings of Israel would triumphantly march into Jerusalem after some military conquest. They would arrive to the cheers of the people of Israel as they rode in their chariots followed by the armies of Israel. This was not to be that kind of march. The Messiah would appear *lowly and riding on a donkey, a colt, the foal of a donkey.* Yet even in His lowly arrival, he would be greeted as the conquering hero as He rode into the city.

The Missing of the Messiah

> The stone which the builders rejected has become the chief cornerstone. This was the LORD'S doing; It is marvelous in our eyes.
>
> -Psalm 118:22

With all of the prophecies of the coming Messiah, with all of the indicators of His arrival, with all of the proofs that He would bring, the nation would be hard hearted and they would miss His coming. Some would miss Him out of blindness and others out of self-imposed blindness, Israel would miss His arrival. Even now Israel has missed their promised one. Even today in this time with all of the evidence of His claims the chosen people of God have rejected her savior.

The Death of the Messiah

The Murder of the Messiah

> My God, My God, why have You forsaken Me? Why are You so far from helping Me, and from the words of My groaning? ...A reproach of men, and despised by the people. All those who see Me ridicule Me; they shoot out the lip, they shake the head, saying, "He trusted in the LORD, let Him rescue Him; Let Him deliver Him, since He delights in Him!" ...Many bulls have surrounded Me; Strong bulls of Bashan

> have encircled Me. They gape at Me with their mouths, like a raging and roaring lion. I am poured out like water, and all My bones are out of joint; My heart is like wax; it has melted within Me. My strength is dried up like a potsherd, and My tongue clings to My jaws; You have brought Me to the dust of death. For dogs have surrounded Me; the congregation of the wicked has enclosed Me. They pierced My hands and My feet; I can count all My bones. They look and stare at Me. They divide My garments among them, And for My clothing they cast lots...
>
> -Psalm 22

Of all of Scripture, this passage looking forward to lonely solitary death of the Messiah is for me the most haunting. He who they welcomed as a triumphant hero, they despised, mocked and murdered. The howl of agony that exudes from this Psalm cuts the reader to his very soul as you morn with those who loved this man, the Messiah. Yet through it all we now know that as the Messiah drew the last of his breaths he cried out to the Father that these should by no means be held accountable for His murder. Even on the cross, He was fulfilling His mission of healing the brokenhearted.

The Miracle of the Messiah
> For You will not leave my soul in Sheol, nor will You allow Your Holy One to see corruption.
>
> -Psalm 16:10

David the King wrote this prophecy. He is in the grave. His body has decomposed. The writer was not writing of himself, he was writing concerning the Messiah. The Messiah, it was said would see no decay. He certainly would die, but He would not see corruption. He would rise again from the pit as one who has conquered death.

The Majesty of the Messiah
> You have ascended on high, You have led captivity captive; You have received gifts among men, even from the rebellious, that the LORD God might dwell there.
>
> -Psalm 68:18

The Messiah would come under certain obvious circumstances, He would be rejected by those who missed Him and he would die. This is what the Word of God has to say concerning His coming. But that is not the end of this great story! He was to raise again from the dead and he was to ascend to Heaven to take His place at the right hand of the Father. He was to be given a place of majesty from which he would return to gather His followers to Himself. Is Jesus the Messiah? Yes, He is.

Is Jesus God?

After having fled Egypt, Moses was serving as a shepherd on the plains of Midian. One day he saw a peculiar sight, a bush that was on fire but was not being consumed. He attentively approached this marvelous sight and was greeted with the very voice of God. That day Moses was given a mission to go back to the home that he had fled some forty years ago. He was to go back, march up to the Pharaoh and demand the release of the children of Israel.

> But Moses said to God, "Who am I that I should go to Pharaoh, and that I should bring the children of Israel out of Egypt?" So He said, "I will certainly be with you. And this shall be a sign to you that I have sent you: When you have brought the people out of Egypt, you shall serve God on this mountain." Then Moses said to God, "Indeed, when I come to the children of Israel and say to them, 'The God of your fathers has sent me to you,' and they say to me, 'What is His name?' what shall I say to them?" And God said to Moses, "**I AM WHO I AM**." And He said, "Thus you shall say to the children of Israel, '**I AM** has sent me to you.'"
>
> -Exodus 3: 11-14

There is much contention over the name of God. Is his name YHWH or is it Jehovah many scholars have argued over this point for years. There is one point that many do agree upon and that is that He identified Himself as I AM, the eternal one.

One day while in the temple Jesus was in conflict with the Jewish religious elite. Jesus said,

> Most assuredly, I say to you, if anyone keeps My word he shall never see death." Then the

Jews said to Him, "Now we know that You have a demon! Abraham is dead, and the prophets; and You say, 'If anyone keeps My word he shall never taste death.' Are You greater than our father Abraham, who is dead? And the prophets are dead. Who do You make Yourself out to be?" Jesus answered, "If I honor Myself, My honor is nothing. It is My Father who honors Me, of whom you say that He is your God. Yet you have not known Him, but I know Him. And if I say, 'I do not know Him,' I shall be a liar like you; but I do know Him and keep His word. Your father Abraham rejoiced to see My day, and he saw it and was glad." Then the Jews said to Him, "You are not yet fifty years old, and have You seen Abraham?" Jesus said to them, "Most assuredly, I say to you, before Abraham was, **I AM**."

-John 8:51-58

Jesus used the divine title and applied it to Himself. Jesus said, in effect, "Do you want to know who I am? Do you really want to know? Ok, I'll tell you who I am. Before Abraham came into being, I am the eternal God." Was this understood by these Jewish leaders? Look at verse 59:

Then they took up stones to throw at Him; but Jesus hid Himself and went out of the temple, going through the midst of them, and so passed by.

Again in conflict with the Jews Jesus said,

I and My Father are one." Then the Jews took up stones again to stone Him. Jesus answered them, "Many good works I have shown you from My Father. For which of those works do you stone Me?" The Jews answered Him,

> saying, "For a good work we do not stone You, but for blasphemy, and because **You**, being a Man, **make Yourself God**."
>
> -John 10:30-33 (see also John 5:17-18)

On the night that Christ was betrayed the temple guard approached Him,

> Jesus therefore, knowing all things that would come upon Him, went forward and said to them, "Whom are you seeking?" They answered Him, "Jesus of Nazareth." Jesus said to them, "**I am**." And Judas, who betrayed Him, also stood with them. Now when He said to them, "**I am**," they drew back and fell to the ground.
>
> -John 18:4-6

Under the power of the truth of His identity His oppressors could not even stand.

This Old Testament calls the Messiah God as well.

> For unto us a **Child is born**, Unto us a Son is given; And the government will be upon His shoulder. And His name will be called Wonderful, Counselor, **Mighty God**, **Everlasting Father**, Prince of Peace.
>
> -Isaiah 9:6

Jesus was in the wilderness for forty days of fasting and being tempted by the devil. The devil showed Him all of the nations of the world and said, I will give them all to you if you fall down and worship me.

> Then Jesus said to him, "Away with you, Satan! For it is written, 'You shall worship the LORD your God, and Him only you shall serve.'"
>
> -Matthew 4:10

This is important because of the next two passages. After Jesus' resurrection, he appeared to His disciples.

> Now Thomas, called the Twin, one of the twelve, was not with them when Jesus came. The other disciples therefore said to him, "We have seen the Lord." So he said to them, "Unless I see in His hands the print of the nails, and put my finger into the print of the nails, and put my hand into His side, I will not believe." And after eight days His disciples were again inside, and Thomas with them. Jesus came, the doors being shut, and stood in the midst, and said, "Peace to you!" Then He said to Thomas, "Reach your finger here, and look at My hands; and reach your hand here, and put it into My side. Do not be unbelieving, but believing." And Thomas answered and said to Him, **"My Lord and my God!"** Jesus said to him, "Thomas, because you have seen Me, you have believed. Blessed are those who have not seen and yet have believed."
>
> -John 20:24-28

The same Jesus who said, "you will worship God and God alone" accepted the worship of Thomas.

In the opening chapter of Hebrews, we see a scene in heaven as God presents the incarnate Christ before the Angels. The author of Hebrews writes,

> For to which of the angels did He ever say: "You are My Son, today I have begotten You"? And again: "I will be to Him a Father, And He shall be to Me a Son"? But when He again brings the firstborn into the world, He says: **"Let all the angels of God worship Him."**
>
> -Hebrew 1:5-6

God the Father calls on the angels to fall down and worship God the Son. Then He goes even further, Look at verse 8 of the same passage.

> But to the Son He says: "Your throne, **O God**, is forever and ever; a scepter of righteousness is the scepter of Your kingdom.

Is Jesus the Messiah? Yes. He is. Is Jesus God? Yes. He is.

Why did Jesus, the Messiah come and die?
Paul the apostle tells us why. First he tells us in Romans 3: 10-18 that man has never been able to attain the level of absolute holiness that God requires. "There is none righteous, no not one." God is absolutely Holy and will not, cannot abide with sin. We are eternally separated from God and at war with him (Romans 5:1). So why did Jesus have to die? In Hebrews 9:22 we read,

> And according to the law almost all things are purified with blood, and without shedding of blood there is no remission.

Christ dies that all men might live. He was the "Lamb of God, which takes away the sin of the world –John 1:29." He came lived a perfect life, He "died for our sins according to the Scriptures, ...He was buried, and ...He rose again the third day according to the Scriptures 1 Cor 15:3-5... This is the reason that Christ became a little lower than the angels and suffered for all mankind. And all one has to do is believe it with the understanding that this saves. As Paul told the jail official in Philippi. "Believe on the Lord Jesus Christ and you will be saved..."

-Acts 16:31.

Theology Proper
(The Doctrine of God)

God is…

Wow! What a bold statement to make. How arrogant it is for us in our finite minds to dare to try to define the infinite God. And, someday as we stand before Him wallowing in our own ignorance, He will look upon us with that patient smile and He will love us. We cannot dare to define Him but we can no doubt explore that which He has revealed to us.

In this study we shall look at the Essence of God, the Attributes of God, the Nature of God and the Triunity of God.

THE ESSENCE OF GOD

First, as always, let us define our terms. Essence is the substance or substances of which a thing consists. To be precise let us say that by the Essence of God we mean that one, self-existent immense, simple spirit of which God exists.

As Dr. Garland Shinn of the Southern California Bible College & Seminary (SCBC&S) said, "God's essence consists of 'spirit stuff.'" God's essence, unlike man's consists of one component, "spirit stuff," which has several characteristics.

What do we mean when we use Dr. Shinn's term "Spirit Stuff?" In the Gospel of Luke we read what a spirit is not:

> Now as they said these things, Jesus Himself stood in the midst of them, and said to them, "Peace to you." But they were terrified and frightened, and supposed they had seen a spirit. And He said to them, "Why are you troubled? And why do doubts arise in your hearts? Behold My hands and My feet, that it is I Myself. **Handle Me and see, for a spirit does not have flesh and bones as you see I have."** When He had said this, He showed them His hands and His feet.
>
> –Luke 24:36-40

A spirit does not have a corporeal body. It does not have flesh and bone. A spirit is not made of flesh and blood either:

> For we do not wrestle against flesh and blood, but against principalities, against powers, against the rulers of the darkness of this age, against spiritual hosts of wickedness in the heavenly places.
>
> –Ephesians 6:12

So, we know what a spirit is not, what is a spirit? A spirit is a real incorporeal immaterial being.

We said that by the Essence of God we mean that *one, self-existent, immense, simple spirit* of which God exists.

God is One:
How many essences are there in the triune God? Look with me at John 10:30:
> I and My Father are one."

There is only one spirit that makes up the triune God. Christ and the Father are one thing not one person, one in essence not one in being. Let's look at the *Shema*, the Jewish confession of faith by which they acknowledged the one true God and His commandments for them.

> Hear, O Israel: The LORD our God, the LORD is one!
> -Deuteronomy 6:4

According to Dr. Garland Shinn,
> "The word 'one' (Heb=*echad*) indicates not 'aloneness of being' but 'unity of essence.' The Hebrew word *'levado'* meaning only or alone is not used here."

In other words, Dr. Shinn is saying that the word *echad* means "one thing." The Shema could read, "Hear, O Israel: YHWH our God, YHWH is one thing." This verse indicates not that there is only one YHWH (which is true) but that YHWH is one thing, or one essence.

God is Self-existent:

By self-existence we mean that the essence of God exists without cause. God is the "uncaused cause" of all things. God showed this to Moses on the plains of Midian. As Moses, the savior of the Nation Israel, the giver of the law, Moses the prophet of God was out tending the sheep he saw a peculiar sight. He saw a bush that was on fire yet not consumed. As he approached he was greeted by the voice of God who told him of his plan to use Moses to rescue the children of Israel from the bondage of Egypt. God told Moses to go to Pharaoh and demand the release of His people. Moses then responded to him and said,

> "Indeed, when I come to the children of Israel and say to them, 'The God of your fathers has sent me to you,' and they say to me, 'What is His name?' what shall I say to them?" And God said to Moses, "**I AM WHO I AM**." And He said, "Thus you shall say to the children of Israel, 'I AM has sent me to you.'"
>
> -Exodus 3:13-14

God said to Moses I AM what I AM. This became the name of God among the Israelites and they referred to this name as "The Eternal One."

In another Scriptural example we find Jesus discussing the resurrection of those who believe and He gives a reason for this:

> For as the Father has life in Himself, so He has granted the Son to have life in Himself,
>
> -John 5:26

God is "continually having life". God has life in the sphere of Himself. This essential life is expressed in the Father, produced in the Son and transferred to believers:

> Most assuredly, I say to you, he who hears My word and believes in Him who sent Me has everlasting life, and shall not come into judgment, but has passed from death into life.
> —John 5:24

And is demonstrated in the resurrection of the dead:

> For as the Father raises the dead and gives life to them, even so the Son gives life to whom He will. For the Father judges no one, but has committed all judgment to the Son, that all should honor the Son just as they honor the Father. He who does not honor the Son does not honor the Father who sent Him. "Most assuredly, I say to you, he who hears My word and believes in Him who sent Me has everlasting life, and shall not come into judgment, but has passed from death into life. Most assuredly, I say to you, the hour is coming, and now is, when the dead will hear the voice of the Son of God; and those who hear will live. For as the Father has life in Himself, so He has granted the Son to have life in Himself, and has given Him authority to execute judgment also, because He is the Son of Man. Do not marvel at this; for the hour is coming in which all who are in the graves will hear His voice and come forth—those who have done good, to the resurrection of life, and those who have done evil, to the resurrection of condemnation.
> -John 5:21-29

God is Immense:

By immensity we are saying that God's essence cannot be contained. Immensity is not to be confused with omnipresence.

> Thus says the LORD: "Heaven is My throne, and earth is My footstool. Where is the house that you will build Me? And where is the place of My rest? For all those things My hand has made, and all those things exist," says the LORD. "But on this one will I look: On him who is poor and of a contrite spirit, and who trembles at My word.
>
> —Isaiah 66:1-2

God is not bigger than His creation. It would be more accurate to say that God is separate from or distinguished from His creation. God's essence is incomparable in size to His creation.

God is a "Simple-Spirit"

> A little boy was working hard on a drawing and his daddy asked him what he was doing. The reply came back, "Drawing a picture of God." His daddy said, "You can't do that, honey. Nobody knows what God looks like." But the little boy was undeterred and continued to draw. He looked at his picture with satisfaction and said very matter-of-factly, "They will in a few minutes."

God is a Simple-Spirit. What in the world do we mean by this statement?

God's essence will never change. It neither ages nor does it whither. God's essence is spirit only, and will never be anything else. God's essence is singular in substance.

> You believe that there **is one God**. You do well.
> Even the demons believe—and tremble!
>
> -James 2:19

They believed that God is one (*in the Greek it would read "God, one is"*). The Demons do not believe the gospel, they believe that God is one essence.

The Attributes of God

What is an attribute? Again, turning to Dr. Garland Shinn,

> The attributes of a thing are the abilities by which it performs and which are consistent with its essence and nature.

Ok, what then are *NOT* attributes? An attribute is not a general characteristic of God, nor a description of God's essence. An attribute is not a description of God's being, nor of God's nature.

What are God's attributes? Dr. Shinn has identified seven attributes of God.

The First of which is goodness. God is Good.

Goodness—Goodness is not to be confused with righteousness. Goodness provides that which is needed to produce happiness.

> He has filled the hungry with good things, And the rich He has sent away empty.
> -Luke 1:53

> Nevertheless He did not leave Himself without witness, in that He did good, gave us rain from heaven and fruitful seasons, filling our hearts with food and gladness."
> -Acts 14:17

In the ultimate sense only God is characteristically good, even though evil men can do good things they are not necessarily good. Jesus was approached by a wealth young man who called out to Him "Good Teacher."

> So Jesus said to him, "Why do you call Me good? No one is good but One, that is, God.
> –Mark 10:18

What a test. Here God is asking someone, why did you call me good, only God is good... Why did you use that description? Do you understand? But, of course the rich young ruler did not understand. Regardless, Jesus teaches us something about our perception... There is only one who is truly good, and that one is God.

> Truly God is good to Israel... -Psalm 73:1

Next is Love. God is Love.

Love— Love is an act of volition and not an emotion. All throughout the New Testament we are commanded to love.

> For the commandments, "You shall not commit adultery," "You shall not murder," "You shall not steal," "You shall not bear false witness," "You shall not covet," and if there is any other commandment, are all summed up in this saying, namely, "You shall love your neighbor as yourself."
> -Romans 13:9

> For all the law is fulfilled in one word, even in this: "You shall love your neighbor as yourself."
> -Galatians 5:14

> Husbands, love your wives and do not be bitter toward them.
>
> –Colossians 3:19

Love is a characteristic of God.

> He who does not love does not know God, for God is love... And we have known and believed the love that God has for us. God is love, and he who abides in love abides in God, and God in him.
>
> -1 John 4:8,16

Next is Truth. God is Truth.

Truth—refers to the quality of being in accord with fact or reality.

The Lord Jesus Christ is truth personified. In teaching His disciples as to who He truly was, and why He had to leave them. Jesus laid it all out for them:

> "Let not your heart be troubled; you believe in God, believe also in Me. In My Father's house are many mansions; if it were not so, I would have told you. I go to prepare a place for you. And if I go and prepare a place for you, I will come again and receive you to Myself; that where I am, there you may be also. And where I go you know, and the way you know." Thomas said to Him, "Lord, we do not know where You are going, and how can we know the way?" Jesus said to him, **"I am the way, the truth, and the life**. No one comes to the Father except through Me.
>
> -John 14:1-6

Jesus was and is in His essence, Truth.

God the Father is characteristically true. Jesus has said His goodbyes to the disciples and He knelt to pray and He said,

> Father, the hour has come. Glorify Your Son, that Your Son also may glorify You, as You have given Him authority over all flesh, that He should give eternal life to as many as You have given Him. And this is eternal life, that they may know You, **the only true God**, and Jesus Christ whom You have sent.
>
> -John 17:1-3

God is righteous:

Righteousness—Righteousness is the quality of consistently acting in accordance with that, which is correct.

Righteousness in an eternal attribute of God:

> Praise the LORD! I will praise the LORD with my whole heart, in the assembly of the upright and in the congregation. The works of the LORD are great, Studied by all who have pleasure in them. His work is honorable and glorious, **and His righteousness endures forever.**
>
> –Psalm 111:1-3

In accordance to His righteousness, God never acts unrighteously:

> Also Your righteousness, O God, is very high, You who have done great things; O God, who is like You?
>
> -Psalm 71:19

God is holy:

Holiness—It denotes the absoluteness, majesty, and awesomeness of the Creator in His distinction from the creature.

The Holiness of God has two facets, the separation of holiness and the conformity to holiness. Holiness involves a separation from:

> Therefore gird up the loins of your mind, be sober, and rest your hope fully upon the grace that is to be brought to you at the revelation of Jesus Christ; as obedient children, **not conforming yourselves to the former lusts**, as in your ignorance"
>
> -1 Peter 1:13-14

Peter is admonishing the Christian recipients of this letter to restrain themselves from the lusts of the world, to separate themselves from the world of sin. Holiness also involves conformity as well. Look at the very next verse:

> "but as He who called you is holy, **you also be holy in all your conduct**, because it is written, "Be holy, for I am holy"
>
> -1 Peter 1:15-16

Just as we are admonished to separate ourselves from the world, we are to conform to the image of God. God is holy in that He separates Himself from anything unlike Himself and conforms perfectly to the purity that He demands of others.

God is Omnipotent:

Omnipotence—Omnipotence means all powerful. The ability to do whatever is deemed necessary.

God is all powerful. There is no power that did not derive from Him. He is the source of all and the end of all. Look at Revelation 1:8, here the Lord Jesus re-introduces Himself to John the Apostle:

> "I am the Alpha and the Omega, *the* Beginning and *the* End," says the Lord, "who is and who was and who is to come, the Almighty."
>
> - Revelation 1:8

> *The* four living creatures, each having six wings, were full of eyes around and within. And they do not rest day or night, saying: "Holy, holy, holy, Lord God Almighty, Who was and is and is to come!"
>
> -Revelation 4:8

In both of these passages the Greek word *Pankrator* is translated "Almighty." God is all powerful in that He is able to do whatever He determines to do, limited only by that which is contrary to His nature.

God is Omniscient:

Omniscience—God is omniscient in that He knows all things instantly and simultaneously, without reference to succession, interval or sequence (See Appendix 1).

> Declaring the end from the beginning, and from ancient times things that are not yet done, saying, 'My counsel shall stand, and I will do all My pleasure,'
>
> –Isaiah 46:10

In chiding the Pharisees Jesus spoke of the infinite knowledge that God has:

> And He said to them, "You are those who justify yourselves before men, but God knows your hearts. For what is highly esteemed among men is an abomination in the sight of God.
> –Luke 16:15

The Nature of God

In general the nature of a thing is the sum total of all that the thing is and does. Essence + Attributes = Nature.

The nature of God consists of six primary things. God is sovereign, free, infinite, eternal, immutable and mobile.

Sovereign

One is sovereign when he is able to express his will without subordination to another in any area of wish or determination. God is sovereign in that He is able to express His volition with reference to the expression of His attributes or essence with no subordination.

> In Him also we have obtained an inheritance, being predestined according to the purpose of **Him who works all things according to the counsel of His will** that we who first trusted in Christ should be to the praise of His glory.
> –Ephesians 1:11-12

> Of His own will He brought us forth by the word of truth, that we might be a kind of firstfruits of His creatures.
> –James 1:18

> There are diversities of gifts, but the same Spirit... But one and the same Spirit works all these things, distributing to each one individually as He wills.
> –1 Cor 12:1, 11

Free

God is free in that He has liberty to express His essence and attributes apart from any inner compulsion or necessity, or from any outward constraint.

> "For who has known the mind of the LORD? Or who has become His counselor?" "Or who has first given to Him and it shall be repaid to him?"
> —Romans 11:34-35

Infinite

God is infinite, as He has no limitations or bounds in any area of His essence or attributes.

> Such knowledge is too wonderful for me; it is high, I cannot attain it. Indeed, the darkness shall not hide from You, but the night shines as the day; the darkness and the light are both alike to You. How precious also are Your thoughts to me, O God! How great is the sum of them! If I should count them, they would be more in number than the sand; when I awake, I am still with You.
> —Psalm 139:6,12,17-18

Eternal

> God is eternal in that He inhabits eternity in such a way as to exist in one whole, indivisible, continual present, so that His is duration without succession, beginning or end.
> —Dr. Garland Shinn

> For thus says the High and Lofty One **Who inhabits eternity**, whose name is Holy: "I dwell

> in the high and holy place, with him who has a contrite and humble spirit, to revive the spirit of the humble,
>
> -Isaiah 57:15

Notice that God does not "Live forever: but instead "Inhabits eternity."

Immutable

God is immutable in that neither His essence nor His attributes change either consciously or unconsciously.

> For when God made a promise to Abraham, because He could swear by no one greater, He swore by Himself, saying, "Surely blessing I will bless you, and multiplying I will multiply you." And so, after he had patiently endured, he obtained the promise. For men indeed swear by the greater, and an oath for confirmation is for them an end of all dispute. Thus God, determining to show more abundantly to the heirs of promise the **immutability** of His counsel, confirmed it by an oath, that by two **immutable** things, in which it is impossible for God to lie, we might have strong consolation, who have fled for refuge to lay hold of the hope set before us.
>
> –Hebrews 6:13-18

> Every good gift and every perfect gift is from above, and comes down from the Father of lights, with whom there is no variation or shadow of turning.
>
> –James 1:17

The Triunity of God

In all of my studies I have searched for *THE* definition of the Trinity. I have come to the conclusion that it is not available. First let me show what others think that the Trinity is. The following is from Walter Martin's *Kingdom of the Cults*.

1. "The doctrine, in brief, is that there **are three gods** in one: 'God the Father, God the Son, and God the Holy Ghost,' all three equal in power, substance, and eternity" (*Let God Be True*, Brooklyn: Watchtower Bible and Tract Society, 1946 ed., 100).

2. "The obvious conclusion is, therefore, that **Satan is the originator of the Trinity doctrine**" (*LGBT*, 101).

3. "Sincere persons who want to know the true God and serve Him find it a bit difficult to love and worship **a complicated, freakish-looking, three-headed God**" (*LGBT*, 102).

4. "The plain truth is that this is another of Satan's attempts to keep God-fearing persons from learning the truth of Jehovah and his Son, Christ Jesus. **No, there is no Trinity**" (*LGBT*, 111).

5. Is Jehovah a Trinity—three persons in one God? **No! Jehovah, the Father, is "the only true God"** (John 17:3; Mark 12:29). Jesus is His firstborn Son, **and he is subject to God** (1 Cor. 11:3). The Father is greater than the Son (John 14:28). **The holy spirit is not a person**; it is God's active force (Gen. 1:2;

> Acts 2:18) (*What Does God Require of Us?*, Brooklyn: Watchtower Bible and Tract Society, 1997, electronic version).

It is infuriatingly clear that the Watchtower Bible and Tract Society does not believe in the Trinity. They charge that the Christian doctrine of the Triune God is a concocted three-headed beast from the pit of hell.

What is the doctrine of the Trinity?

Again I refer to Dr. Shinn,
> By Trinity we mean that God is one eternal, self-existent, immense and simple spirit Who is individualized by three distinct and identifiable persons designated the Father, Son and Holy Spirit.

When asked about the Trinity, I operate on the scientific principle of the following proposal:

If we can find that there are three persons in Scripture who are all called God and if we can show that there is only one God, then the three persons are the one God. Or in other words, three things that are equal to the same thing are equal to each other.

Therefore, it is our mission to prove that there is a person in Scripture that is called the Father and that He is also called God. Secondly we will investigate the proposition that there is a person in Scripture called the Son and that He is identified as God. Then we will establish the fact that the Holy Spirit is called God. Finally, we will attempt to show that there is only one God.

God the Father:
For He received from **God** the **Father** honor and glory when such a voice came to Him from the Excellent Glory: "This is My beloved Son, in whom I am well pleased."
-II Peter 1:17

> Do not labor for the food which perishes, but for the food which endures to everlasting life, which the Son of Man will give you, because **God** the **Father** has set His seal on Him."
> -John 6:27

> yet for us there is one **God**, the **Father**, of whom are all things, and we for Him; and one Lord Jesus Christ, through whom are all things, and through whom we live.
> -1 Cor 8:6

God the Son:
After having fled Egypt, Moses was serving as a shepherd on the plains of Midian. One day he saw a peculiar sight, a bush that was on fire but was not being consumed. He attentively approached this marvelous sight and was greeted with the very voice of God. That day Moses was given a mission to go back to the home that he had fled some forty years ago. He was to go back, march up to the Pharaoh and demand the release of the children of Israel.

> But Moses said to God, "Who am I that I should go to Pharaoh, and that I should bring the children of Israel out of Egypt?" So He said, "I will certainly be with you. And this shall be a sign to you that I have sent you: When you have brought the people out of Egypt, you shall serve God on this mountain." Then Moses said to God, "Indeed, when I come to the children of

> Israel and say to them, 'The God of your fathers has sent me to you,' and they say to me, 'What is His name?' what shall I say to them?" And God said to Moses, "**I AM WHO I AM**." And He said, "Thus you shall say to the children of Israel, '**I AM** has sent me to you.'"
>
> -Exodus 3: 11-14

There is much contention over the name of God. Is his name YHWH or is it Jehovah? Many scholars have argued over this point for years. There is one point that many do agree upon and that is that He identified Himself as I AM, the eternal one.

One day while in the temple Jesus was in conflict with the Jewish religious elite. Jesus said,

> Most assuredly, I say to you, if anyone keeps My word he shall never see death." Then the Jews said to Him, "Now we know that You have a demon! Abraham is dead, and the prophets; and You say, 'If anyone keeps My word he shall never taste death.' Are You greater than our father Abraham, who is dead? And the prophets are dead. Who do You make Yourself out to be?" Jesus answered, "If I honor Myself, My honor is nothing. It is My Father who honors Me, of whom you say that He is your God. Yet you have not known Him, but I know Him. And if I say, 'I do not know Him,' I shall be a liar like you; but I do know Him and keep His word. Your father Abraham rejoiced to see My day, and he saw it and was glad." Then the Jews said to Him, "You are not yet fifty years old, and have You seen Abraham?" Jesus said to them, "Most assuredly, I say to you, before Abraham was, **I AM**."
>
> -John 8:51-58

Jesus used the divine title and applied it to Himself. Jesus said, in effect, "Do you want to know who I am? Do you really want to know? Ok, I'll tell you who I am. Before Abraham came into being, I am the eternal God." Was this understood by these Jewish leaders? Look at verse 59:

> Then they took up stones to throw at Him; but Jesus hid Himself and went out of the temple, going through the midst of them, and so passed by.

Again in conflict with the Jews Jesus said,

> I and My Father are one." Then the Jews took up stones again to stone Him. Jesus answered them, "Many good works I have shown you from My Father. For which of those works do you stone Me?" The Jews answered Him, saying, "For a good work we do not stone You, but for blasphemy, and because **You**, being a Man, **make Yourself God**."
> -John 10:30-33 (see also John 5:17-18)

On the night that Christ was betrayed the temple guard approached Him,

> Jesus therefore, knowing all things that would come upon Him, went forward and said to them, "Whom are you seeking?" They answered Him, "Jesus of Nazareth." Jesus said to them, "**I am**." And Judas, who betrayed Him, also stood with them. Now when He said to them, "**I am**," they drew back and fell to the ground.
> -John 18:4-6

Under the power of the truth of His identity His oppressors could not even stand.

This Old Testament calls the Messiah God as well.

> For unto us a **Child is born**, Unto us a Son is given; And the government will be upon His shoulder. And His name will be called Wonderful, Counselor, **Mighty God**, **Everlasting Father**, Prince of Peace.
>
> -Isaiah 9:6

Jesus was in the wilderness for forty days of fasting and being tempted by the devil. The devil showed Him all of the nations of the world and said, I will give them all to you if you fall down and worship me.

> Then Jesus said to him, "Away with you, Satan! For it is written, 'You shall worship the LORD your God, and Him only you shall serve.'"
>
> -Matthew 4:10

This is important because of the next two passages. After Jesus' resurrection, he appeared to His disciples.

> Now Thomas, called the Twin, one of the twelve, was not with them when Jesus came. The other disciples therefore said to him, "We have seen the Lord." So he said to them, "Unless I see in His hands the print of the nails, and put my finger into the print of the nails, and put my hand into His side, I will not believe." And after eight days His disciples were again inside, and Thomas with them. Jesus came, the doors being shut, and stood in the midst, and

> said, "Peace to you!" Then He said to Thomas, "Reach your finger here, and look at My hands; and reach your hand here, and put it into My side. Do not be unbelieving, but believing." And Thomas answered and said to Him, **"My Lord and my God!"** Jesus said to him, "Thomas, because you have seen Me, you have believed. Blessed are those who have not seen and yet have believed."
>
> -John 20:24-28

The same Jesus who said, "you will worship God and God alone" accepted the worship of Thomas.

In the opening chapter of Hebrews, we see a scene in heaven as God presents the incarnate Christ before the Angels. The author of Hebrews writes,

> For to which of the angels did He ever say: "You are My Son, today I have begotten You"? And again: "I will be to Him a Father, And He shall be to Me a Son"? But when He again brings the firstborn into the world, He says: **"Let all the angels of God worship Him."**
>
> -Hebrew 1:5-6

God the Father calls on the angels to fall down and worship God the Son. Then He goes even further, Look at verse 8 of the same passage.

> But to the Son He says: "Your throne, **O God**, is forever and ever; a scepter of righteousness is the scepter of Your kingdom.

God the Holy Spirit:
The Holy Spirit is a person-
> Now in the church that was at Antioch there were certain prophets and teachers: Barnabas, Simeon who was called Niger, Lucius of Cyrene, Manaen who had been brought up with Herod the tetrarch, and Saul. As they ministered to the Lord and fasted, the **Holy Spirit** said, "Now separate to Me Barnabas and Saul for the **work to which I have called them.**"
>
> -Acts 13:1-2

The Holy Spirit is called God-
> But a certain man named Ananias, with Sapphira his wife, sold a possession. And he kept back part of the proceeds, his wife also being aware of it, and brought a certain part and laid it at the apostles' feet. But Peter said, "Ananias, why has Satan filled your heart **to lie to the Holy Spirit** and keep back part of the price of the land for yourself? While it remained, was it not your own? And after it was sold, was it not in your own control? Why have you conceived this thing in your heart? **You have not lied to men but to God.**"
>
> -Acts 5:1-4

One God:
> "You are My witnesses," says the LORD, "And My servant whom I have chosen, That you may know and believe Me, And understand that I am He. **Before Me there was no God formed, Nor shall there be after Me.**
>
> -Isaiah 43:10

"Thus says the LORD, the King of Israel, And his Redeemer, the LORD of hosts: 'I am the First and I am the Last; Besides **Me there is no God**.

—Isaiah 44:6

"Look to Me, and be saved, All you ends of the earth! **For I am God, and there is no other**.

-Isaiah 45:22

For there is one God and one Mediator between God and men, the Man Christ Jesus, who gave Himself a ransom for all, to be testified in due time, for which I was appointed a preacher and an apostle—I am speaking the truth in Christ and not lying—a teacher of the Gentiles in faith and truth.

—1 Tim 2: 5-7

Conclusion:

It is clear from Scripture that there are three person's all called God. And it is clear that there is only one God. Therefore the three persons are the one God.

Pneumatology
(The Doctrine of the Holy Spirit)

"We have not so much as heard whether there is a Holy Spirit."

–Acts 19:2

One of the least explored doctrines must be Pneumatology. We all call on Him, we all attribute wonderful works to Him we all praise Him. But what do we know about Him? The goal of this writing is to first establish who He is. Secondly, explore what He does and discover our relationship to Him.

WHO IS THE HOLY SPIRIT

He is GOD. In defining our terms we must determine who or what we are discussing. We must determine who the Holy Spirit is. First is He a he? There has been much ink spilled by those who would deny not only the deity of the Holy Spirit but even deny His personality.

Is the Holy Spirit a person?

Person- A person is an entity that has intellect, will and emotion. Using our definition, let us determine, from Scripture if indeed the Holy Spirit has intellect, will and emotion, thus determining if He is a person.

***Intellect-* Does the Holy Spirit have intellect?**

Jesus in the upper room discourse, taught the disciples concerning the ministry of the Holy Spirit and what His function would be.

> Nevertheless I tell you the truth. It is to your advantage that I go away; for if I do not go away, the Helper will not come to you; but if I depart, I will send Him to you. And when He has come, He will convict the world of sin, and of righteousness, and of judgment... v.13 However, when He, the Spirit of truth, has come, He will guide you into all truth; for He will not speak on His own authority, but whatever He hears He will speak; and He will tell you things to come.
> –John 16 7-8, 13

Notice first that he convicts. Though His intellect here is not concrete it is strongly inferred. First He must have the intellectual capacity to discern sin. Followed by a methodology of conviction. This is not an activity that some mindless power or force could accomplish. He determines between sin and righteousness and shows an awareness of the coming judgment.

Secondly Jesus shows that He teaches. *"He will guide you into all truth."* This is not a simple pathway leading to truth, this is a demonstration of the illuminating ministry of the Holy Spirit (See Illumination in Bibliology).

Notice again that He speaks. *"...for He will not speak on His own authority, but whatever He hears He will speak; and He will tell you things to come."* The Holy Spirit has the obvious ability to determine what to speak and what not to speak. He even has His own thoughts and restrains them.

It is abundantly clear that the Holy Spirit teaches, discerns, convicts, thinks and speaks. This is indisputable Biblical evidence for the intellect of the Holy Spirit. Does the Holy Spirit have intellect? Yes.

ized="">*Will*- Does the Holy Spirit have will?

After having rested for some time in Antioch, Paul was commissioned back to the mission field.

> Now in the church that was at Antioch there were certain prophets and teachers: Barnabas, Simeon who was called Niger, Lucius of Cyrene, Manaen who had been brought up with Herod the tetrarch, and Saul. ²As they ministered to the Lord and fasted, the Holy Spirit said, "Now separate to Me Barnabas and Saul for the work to which I have called them." ³Then, having fasted and prayed, and laid hands on them, they sent them away. So, being sent

> out by the Holy Spirit, they went down to Seleucia, and from there they sailed to Cyprus.
> -Acts 13:1-4

Here the Holy Spirit demonstrated independent thought, the ability to speak and His own will. Whose work were they called to? *"The Holy Spirit said, 'Now separate to Me Barnabas and Saul for the work to which I have called them.'"* It was the Holy Spirit who called them to a certain work, through an exercise of His own will. He identified the particular persons that He wanted for a particular job. He then communicated His will to them and He sent them on their way, *"So, being sent out by the Holy Spirit, they went down to Seleucia, and from there they sailed to Cyprus."* Does the Holy Spirit have a will? Yes.

Emotion- **Does the Holy Spirit have emotion?**

Paul the apostle in his writings to the church of Ephesus, was teaching the saints how to live together according to their new nature. He asked them not to lie, steal or gossip. Then Paul explains a certain result of "evil speaking".

> Therefore, putting away lying, "Let each one of you speak truth with his neighbor," for we are members of one another. "Be angry, and do not sin" do not let the sun go down on your wrath, nor give place to the devil. Let him who stole steal no longer, but rather let him labor, working with his hands what is good, that he may have something to give him who has need. Let no corrupt word proceed out of your mouth, but what is good for necessary edification, that it may impart grace to the hearers. **And do not grieve the Holy Spirit of God**, by whom you were sealed for the day of redemption. Let all bitterness, wrath, anger, clamor, and evil

> speaking be put away from you, with all malice. And be kind to one another, tenderhearted, forgiving one another, even as God in Christ forgave you.
>
> -Ephesians 4:25-32

According to Webster's Dictionary "grieve" means "to cause to be sorrowful; distress." Sorrow and distress are emotions. When we, by our ungodly behavior grieve the Holy Spirit, we hurt Him. We cause Him sorrow. Does the Holy Spirit have emotion? Yes.

Is the Holy Spirit a person? Yes.

IS THE HOLY SPIRIT GOD?

During the first century, there was much need among the new Christian community. As a result many Christians sold their possessions for the purpose of sharing the funds with those many in need. In Acts 5:1-4 we read:

> But a certain man named Ananias, with Sapphira his wife, sold a possession. And he kept back *part* of the proceeds, his wife also being aware *of it,* and brought a certain part and laid *it* at the apostles' feet. But Peter said, "Ananias, why has Satan filled your heart to lie to the Holy Spirit and keep back *part* of the price of the land for yourself? While it remained, was it not your own? And after it was sold, was it not in your own control? Why have you conceived this thing in your heart? You have not lied to men but to God."

Peter rebuked Ananias for lying to the Holy Spirit. Again we see the personality of the Holy Spirit being demonstrated. Peter then clarifies the depth of the sin of Ananias. He stated,

"You have not lied to men but to God." Peter himself identified the Holy Spirit as God.
Is the Holy Spirit God? Yes.

WHAT DOES THE HOLY SPIRIT DO?

Biblically speaking, we are able to determine that the Holy Spirit is indeed a person and that he is at the very least called God in the inspired inerrant Scriptures. Now what does he do? In this portion of the study we are going to look at five functions of the Spirit in the life of a believer, the baptism of the Holy Spirit, indwelling, sealing, gift distribution and filling.

The Baptism of the Holy Spirit
Is the baptism of the Holy Spirit a "second blessing" that results in every believer speaking in an unknown tongue, giving him power and authority and a level of achieved holiness? I used to think so. But is that what the Bible teaches about it? No.

Romans 6:1-3 says this of the baptism of the Holy Spirit:

> What shall we say then? Shall we continue in sin that grace may abound? Certainly not! How shall we who died to sin live any longer in it? Or do you not know that as many of us as were baptized into Christ Jesus were baptized into His death?

Paul is writing of the moment of belief when a sinner becomes a saint when one who is at war with the Almighty finds a peace and joy in his spirit. We are baptized not into the Holy Spirit, but by the Holy Spirit into the body of Christ.

Paul clarifies this concept in his first letter to the Corinthians:

> For as the body is one and has many members, but all the members of that one body, being many, are one body, so also is Christ. **For by one Spirit we were all baptized into one body**—whether Jews or Greeks, whether slaves or free—and have all been made to drink into one Spirit. For in fact the body is not one member but many.
>
> -1 Cor 12:12-14

Paul makes it clear that the baptizing work of the Holy Spirit has nothing to do with any of the gifts. It is much more than that. It is the placing into the body one who was once an enemy. Who better could understand that transition of going from enemy to family than Paul. That is why he wrote to the Galatians and said,

> For **you are all sons of God through faith in Christ Jesus**. For as many of you as were baptized into Christ have put on Christ. There is neither Jew nor Greek, there is neither slave nor free, there is neither male nor female; for you are all one in Christ Jesus. And if you are Christ's, then you are Abraham's seed, and heirs according to the promise.
>
> –Galatians 3:26-29

When does the baptism of the Holy Spirit take place? At the moment of one's conversion. What do we mean by the baptism of the Holy Spirit? It is that instantaneous, glorious moment when we are taken from the body of evil and placed into the body of Christ, plunged into this new family, baptized into His suffering and death to never emerge.

The Indwelling of the Holy Spirit

What is the indwelling of the Holy Spirit? Does this occur to all men for a time and the He departs. What did David mean when he prayed, "Take not your Holy Spirit from me"?

Jesus in His introduction of the Holy Spirit stated:

> And I will pray the Father, and He will give you another Helper, that He may abide with you forever—the Spirit of truth, whom the world cannot receive, because it neither sees Him nor knows Him; but you know Him, **for He dwells with you and will be in you**.
>
> –John 14:16-17

Jesus told the disciples "you know Him." He has been here *with* you. But when I go He will indwell you. He will take up residence within you and He will remain in you not to leave.

A person is not a Christian if the Holy Spirit does not indwell him.

> But you are not in the flesh but in the Spirit, if indeed the Spirit of God dwells in you. Now if anyone does not have the Spirit of Christ, he is not His.
>
> –Romans 8:9

Paul wrote to the carnal Corinthians and pleaded with them to relinquish their sinful ways, saying:

> Or do you not know that your body is the temple of the Holy Spirit *who is* in you, whom you have from God, and you are not your own? For you were bought at a price; therefore glorify

God in your body and in your spirit, which are God's. –1 Corinthians 6:18-20

The Sealing of the Holy Spirit
The sealing of the Holy Spirit is the work that God carries out on behalf of the believer to secure his salvation:

> Now He who establishes us with you in Christ and has anointed us is God, **who also has sealed us and given us the Spirit in our hearts as a guarantee.**
> –2 Corinthians 1:21-22

> In Him you also trusted, after you heard the word of truth, the Gospel of your salvation; in whom also, having believed, you were sealed with the Holy Spirit of promise, **who is the guarantee of our inheritance until the redemption** of the purchased possession, to the praise of His glory.
> –Ephesians 1:13-14

Second Corinthians 1:22 says God *"sealed us and gave us the Spirit in our hearts as a pledge."* The Holy Spirit is given to the person who believes in Christ as a seal, identifying the believer as belonging to God. This also occurs at the moment of conversion.

THE GIFTS OF THE HOLY SPIRIT

In first Corinthians 12:4-7,14 Paul instructs the believers concerning the gifts of the Holy spirit.

> There are diversities of gifts, but the same Spirit. There are differences of ministries, but the same Lord. And there are diversities of activities, but it is the same God who works all

> in all. But the manifestation of the Spirit is given to each one for the profit of all... But one and the same Spirit works all these things, distributing to each one individually as He wills.

Paul instructs on a couple of key points here. First he introduces the concepts of varied gifts but ties them all to the same Holy Spirit. There are many different abilities that God gives, but the Holy Spirit gives them all. Then he tackles the next weighty issue. *"It is the same God who works all in all. But the manifestation of the Spirit is given to each one for the profit of all."* Not only does Paul here reaffirm the sources of the gift, "the same God" but he also gives us the reason for them. These gifts, says Paul are given to each for the profit of all. They are to be exercised within the body for the edification of one another. Thirdly, Paul touches on a point that we have previously discussed, that the gifts are distributed according to the will of the Holy Spirit.

The Filling of the Holy Spirit
The basis for the filling of the Spirit is given to us in Paul's letter to the church in Ephesus:

> And do not be drunk with wine, in which is dissipation; but be filled with the Spirit,
> -Ephesians 5:18

The command to be filled with the Spirit is given in contrast to the warning "do not get drunk with wine." Drunkenness shows the inability of the person to control himself. The nature of the Christian's life is to be in contrast to the nature of the uncontrolled drunk. The meaning of "filled" is "control." "The indwelling Spirit of God is the One who should continually control the life of the believer." Another contrast can be noted between the spiritual believer and the carnal believer (1 Cor. 2:9-3:4). "The carnal man is the man who lives by the power of the flesh, according to the dictates of the flesh, and the spiritual man is the man who lives by the power of the Spirit."

Soteriology
(The Doctrine of Salvation)

Payson, when dying, expressed himself with great earnestness respecting the grace of God as exercised in saving the lost and seemed particularly affected that it should be bestowed on one so ill-deserving as himself. "Oh, how sovereign! Oh, how sovereign! Grace is the only thing that can make us like God. I might be dragged through heaven, earth, and hell, and I should still be the same sinful, polluted wretch, unless God himself renews and cleanses me[1]."

---

[1] Charles Haddon Spurgeon, The Quotable Spurgeon, (Wheaton: Harold Shaw Publishers, Inc, 1990)

What is salvation? What do these evangelicals mean by an *assurance*? When asked the evangelistic question, "When you die, are you sure of where you will go?" You will receive a variety of answers. You will hear "no one can be sure..." or "Well I have been a good person..." or "I have done more good than bad..."

But as Christians we have certain important truths that we are told.

The power of the Gospel

First, our salvation is based not on us but on the power of God:

> For I am not ashamed of the Gospel of Christ, **for it is the power of God** to salvation for everyone who believes, for the Jew first and also for the Greek.
>
> –Romans 1:16

The Gospel of Christ is the power of God unto salvation. Why it that? Look at verse 17:

> For in it the righteousness of God is revealed from faith to faith; as it is written, "The just shall live by faith."
>
> --Romans 1:17

The Gospel of Christ is the power of God unto salvation because in it the righteousness of God is revealed. The Gospel reveals to man and heaven the depths of God's righteousness. It demonstrated the boundlessness of God's grace and His mercy. So, our salvation is based on the power of God.

The Assurance of the Gospel

The second important point is that once we are saved we know, without a doubt that we are saved.

> These things I have written to you who believe in the name of the Son of God, that you may know that you have eternal life, and that you may continue to believe in the name of the Son of God.
>
> −1 John 5:13

John first identifies who he is writing to, "These things I have written to **you who believe in the name of the Son of God**." He is writing to believers. Next he tells us why he is writing to believers, "**that you may know** that you have eternal life." John is writing to those who have believed in the Gospel message and he says to them you can have an assurance that your salvation is both real and complete. The writer of Hebrews puts it this way, "...Jesus, the author and finisher of our faith..." Hebrews 12:2.

I was recently teaching verse by verse through the book of Romans at the Donavon State Prison in San Diego California. I have very few rules in my class; these men are Christians and need little direction. One rule that I have is that I do not want to know the crimes for which you are incarcerated. One day while teaching from Romans 5:1 on the peace we now have with God and His amazing grace, one inmate blurted out, "I am here because I killed my mother with a hammer. How can I know that I am saved?" The class was stunned, as was I, but in the power of Christ I summoned an answer. I looked at this huge man dressed in the clothes of a convicted killer with tears streaming down his cheeks, I put my hand on his shoulder, and I asked, "Before you came to Christ, how did you feel when you sinned?" He responded saying, "I didn't care." I asked, "and now how do you feel?" He said, "It tears me up inside."

I looked in to his questioning eyes and I said, "Brother, that is because the Spirit of God now dwells within you. That is because you are one of His. You have been forgiven for your crime, for all of your sins and are now righteous in His eyes." That is the good news of the Gospel. I saw that pain leave that man and I saw how Christ is still setting the captives free.

The Eternity of the Gospel

I was raised in a denomination that taught that salvation was a free gift of grace but the keeping of it once attained was contingent on your behavior. In other words God saved you by His grace but he ended His involvement at that point and left you to fend for yourself. As a result I had to get "re-saved" every Sunday evening. I had not been taught of God's sovereign ability to keep his children free. I had not studied the total Word of God. I had not understood the word of the Lord Jesus when He said,

> And I give them eternal life, and they shall never perish; neither shall anyone snatch them out of My hand.
> –John 10:28

Jesus was answering the Jews who were to reject Him and He said, look, those who are mine, I will keep. He basically said, you do not understand these things because you are not of mine.

Paul the Apostle understood this great truth and endeavored to teach it to the Christians in Rome.

> There is therefore now no condemnation to those who are in Christ Jesus, who do not walk according to the flesh, but according to the Spirit. –Romans 8:1

C.H. Spurgeon tells the story of an old simple farmer who understood this truth better than most:

> There is an old ploughman in the country I sometimes talk with, and he often says some precious things. He said to me one day, "The other day, sir, the Devil was tempting me and I tried to answer him; but I found he was an old lawyer and understood the law a great deal better than I did, so I gave over and would not argue with him any more; so I said to him, 'What do you trouble me for?' 'Why,' said he, 'about your soul.' 'Oh!' said I, 'that is no business of mine; I have given my soul over into the hand of Christ; I have transferred everything to him; if you want an answer to your doubts and queries, you must apply to my Advocate.'"
>
> --Charles H. Spurgeon

The Simplicity of the Gospel

> When Dionysius, the tyrant, sent Lysander some rich Sicilian garments for his daughters, Lysander refused them, alleging that such fine clothes would make them look homely in comparison. The truth of God is so comely in itself that the trappings of oratory are far more likely to lessen its glory than to increase it. Paul said that he preached the Gospel "not with wisdom of words, lest the cross of Christ should be made of none effect.[2]"

When the Apostle Paul opened his letter to the Romans, he began his teaching by declaring the power behind his message:

---

[2] Charles Haddon Spurgeon, The Quotable Spurgeon, (Wheaton: Harold Shaw Publishers, Inc, 1990)

> For I am not ashamed of the Gospel of Christ, for it is the power of God to salvation for everyone who believes, for the Jew first and also for the Greek.
>
> –Romans 1:16

He said, the power behind the Gospel is the power of God. That is where the power came from, but there was something else that Paul wrote here. He opened this thought by saying, *"I am not ashamed of the Gospel of Christ."* This leads us to ask the question, "What is there to be ashamed of?" The Gospel is simple. There are no incantations, no physical requirements; there is nothing that one can do to earn the salvation granted through the Gospel. It is simple faith that saves. Paul unveils the essential elements of the Gospel in his first letter to the Corinthians:

> Moreover, brethren, I declare to you the Gospel which I preached to you, which also you received and in which you stand, by which also you are saved, if you hold fast that word which I preached to you—unless you believed in vain. For I delivered to you first of all that which I also received: that Christ died for our sins according to the Scriptures, and that He was buried, and that He rose again the third day according to the Scriptures, and that He was seen by Cephas, then by the twelve.
>
> –1 Corinthians 15:1-5

This is the Gospel that is the power of God unto salvation, the Gospel that Paul determined not to be ashamed of. He begins by assuring them that this was THE Gospel, the one that they believed, in which they stand and by which they were saved. Notice the line *"unless you believed in vain."* The Gospel saves you when you believe it for the purpose of being saved.

Paul said here it is in all of its glory. 1. Christ died for our sins according to the Scriptures. 2. He was buried as evidence of His death. 3. He rose from the dead, according to the Scriptures and was seen by many witnesses. That is the Gospel. There is no more. Notice that it does not say anything about being baptized, or speaking in tongues. It does not require the performance of seven rituals or any other work. It does not even require that a "sinner's prayer" be prayed, or the aisle of a Baptist church be walked. It is simply a matter of believing.

The Working of the Gospel

> If I had the wisdom of Solomon, the patience of John, the meekness of Moses, the strength of Samson, the obedience of Abraham, the compassion of Joseph, the tears of Jeremiah, the poetic skill of David, the prophetic voice of Elijah, the courage of Daniel, the greatness of John the Baptist, the endurance and love of Paul, I would still need redemption through Christ's blood, the forgiveness of sin.
>
> --R. L. Wheeler[3]

The work of salvation is not simple. Though the Gospel is simple enough for a child to believe, the mysteries of the Gospel have dumbfounded theologians for centuries.

Knowing that we are going into over-charted waters, let us define a very few key terms:

GRACE. When God gives us that which we do not deserve.

---

[3] Edythe Draper, Draper's Book of Quotations for the Christian World (Wheaton: Tyndale House Publishers, Inc., 1992).

JUSTIFICATION. Comes from a Greek concept meaning "to declare righteous." It is a legal act wherein God pronounces that the believing sinner has been credited with all the virtues of Jesus Christ. Whereas forgiveness is the negative aspect of salvation, meaning the subtraction of human sin, justification is the positive aspect meaning, the addition of divine righteousness.

MERCY. When God does not give us that which we do deserve.

PROPITIATION. Comes from a Greek concept meaning "to appease or to atone" and stresses that the holiness of God was fully satisfied, His wrath appeased, and His righteous demands were met through the atoning death of Christ.

REDEMPTION. Comes from several Greek terms that cumulatively mean "to set free by the payment of a price." It emphasizes that through His death, Christ set the believer free from enslavement to sin.

SANCTIFICATION. Comes from a Greek verb meaning "to set apart." It is used in two ways: (1) the believer is positionally sanctified; he stands sanctified before God; (2) the believer grows in progressive sanctification in daily spiritual experience.

The problem:

As we have already discovered, Man is totally and completely depraved, evil and given over to sin (See Hamartiology). He has no hope of salvation apart from Christ. Our very best is not good enough.

> But we are all like an unclean thing, and all **our righteousnesses are like filthy rags**; we all fade as a leaf, and our iniquities, like the wind, have taken us away.
> --Isaiah 64:6

When a sinner compares himself with those paraded on the evening news He fares very well. However when he looks at his heart in the light of God's word he begins to see the dirt and filth left on him by a life apart from God.

> "No man knows how bad he is until he has tried very hard to be good.[4]" --C.S. Lewis

No truthful man can say that he is without sin in thought word and deed. Paul makes this abundantly clear:

> As it is written: **"There is none righteous, no, not one**; there is none who understands; **There is none who seeks after God.** They have all turned aside; **they have together become unprofitable; There is none who does good, no, not one."** "Their throat is an open tomb; **with their tongues they have practiced deceit**"; "The poison of asps is under their lips"; "Whose mouth is full of cursing and bitterness." "Their feet are swift to shed blood; Destruction

---

[4] Lewis, C.S., *The Quotable Lewis*, (Wheaton: Tyndale, 1989).

> and misery are in their ways; And the way of peace they have not known." **"There is no fear of God** before their eyes."
>
> --Romans 3:10-18

> But now the righteousness of God apart from the law is revealed, being witnessed by the Law and the Prophets, even the righteousness of God, through faith in Jesus Christ, to all and on all who believe. For there is no difference; for all have sinned and fall short of the glory of God,
>
> -Romans 3:21-23

This leaves little room for debate. There is none who is righteous.

The Requirement:

From the earliest times, God's requirement for man has been laid out:

> and that you may remember and do all My commandments, and **be holy** for your God. I am the LORD your God, who brought you out of the land of Egypt, to be your God: I am the LORD your God."
>
> --Numbers 15:40-41

God demands absolute holiness. Man is absolutely unholy. Man cannot attain absolute holiness. God therefore provided a means to attain that holiness that He requires.

The Solution:

> But God demonstrates His own love toward us, in that while we were still sinners, Christ died for us.
>
> –Romans 5:8

We were at war with God, not even seeking peace. And God, the ultimate victor, offered us peace instead of annihilation. The means of that peace was His Son Jesus Christ. Through His blood that the filthy are *justified*.

> But now the righteousness of God apart from the law is revealed, being witnessed by the Law and the Prophets, even the righteousness of God, through faith in Jesus Christ, to all and on all who believe. For there is no difference; for all have sinned and fall short of the glory of God, being **justified** freely by His grace through the redemption that is in Christ Jesus,
>
> --Romans 3:21-24

> Therefore, having been justified by faith, we have peace with God through our Lord Jesus Christ,
>
> --Romans 5:1

There is but one cure to the terminal disease called sin, and that is the grace of the Lord Jesus Christ.

The Response:

During a missionary journey, Paul the Apostle and Silas his fellow worker in the cause of the Gospel were jailed in a small Roman colony in a district of Macedonia:

> But at midnight Paul and Silas were praying and singing hymns to God, and the prisoners were listening to them. Suddenly there was a great earthquake, so that the foundations of the prison were shaken; and immediately all the doors were opened and everyone's chains were loosed. And the keeper of the prison, awaking from sleep and seeing the prison doors open, supposing the prisoners had fled, drew his sword and was about to kill himself. But Paul called with a loud voice, saying, "Do yourself no harm, for we are all here." Then he called for a light, ran in, and fell down trembling before Paul and Silas. And he brought them out and said, **"Sirs, what must I do to be saved?" So they said, "Believe on the Lord Jesus Christ, and you will be saved, you and your household."** Then they spoke the word of the Lord to him and to all who were in his house…and he rejoiced, having believed…
>
> -Acts 16:25-34

This Greek official saw not only the power of God displayed buy the mercy of Christ displayed. These men could well have fled and he would have been held accountable. I believe that it was as much the fact that they were still there as anything that caused him to call on the Lord Jesus for salvation.

These words of Paul, "Believe on the Lord Jesus Christ and you will be saved…" have as much power in this millennium as they did when they were first spoken to a broken suicidal Macedonian jailer.

Bibliology
(The Doctrine of the Bible)

They lie on the table side by side, The Holy Bible and the TV guide. One is well worn and cherished with pride, Not the Bible ... but the TV guide. One is used daily to help folks decide, No, not the Bible... but the TV guide. As the pages are turned, what shall they see, Oh, what does it matter, turn on the TV. Then confusion reigns, they can't all agree, On what they should watch on the old TV. So they open the book in which they confide, No, not the Bible... but the TV guide. The Word of God is seldom read, Maybe a verse as they fall into bed. Exhausted and sleepy and tired as can be, Not from reading the Bible... from watching

> TV. So then back to the table side by side, Lie the Holy Bible and the TV guide. No time for prayer, no time for the Word, The plan of Salvation is seldom heard. But forgiveness of sin, so full and free, Is found in the Bible... not on TV.

The Apostle Paul, in writing to a young pastor named Timothy, emphasized the extreme importance of a thorough and constant study of the Word of God. "Be diligent to present yourself approved to God, a worker who does not need to be ashamed, rightly dividing the word of truth" –2 Timothy 2:15. The Greek word translated diligent, *spoudadzo*, is a word of intensity. *Thayer's Greek Definitions* defines it this way:

1) to hasten, make haste
2) to exert one's self, endeavor, give diligence

The idea behind Paul's choice of this word was one of determination, imperativeness, fortitude and diligence. Paul told Timothy later in the same letter that the Word of God was the power necessary to endure persecution and defeat the wiles of evil men (2 Timothy 3:12-17). We see in our day that there is a steering away from The Word, and as a result our churches are filled with halfhearted, immature, dying Christians.

Glossary
In order to best conduct a study of the Doctrine of the Bible, it is first imperative to define the terminology that is common to this area of theology. For this reason, the glossary precedes any discussion of the actual teaching of Bibliology.

Animation- That element of life that is inherent in the Bible as in no other book (Hebrews 4:12).

Authority- The right, inherent in God and vested in Scripture, to demand response or obedience (James 1:22).

Autographs- Those earliest writings of the original authors of Scripture. There are currently no true autographs available.

Bibliology- The doctrine of the Bible. The theological study of what the Bible says about itself. This includes revelation, Inscripturation, inspiration, authority, canonicity, animation, interpretation, preservation and translation.

Canonicity- The process of recognizing which books are intended by God to rule or measure our lives (Luke 24:44-45). A term used relative to the sixty-six books of the Bible, indicating they have passed the tests used to determine their inspiration and inclusion in the body of sacred Scripture.

Dual Authorship- The original autographs (hand-written documents produced by the original writer) were verbally inspired (in every word, every letter, and every part of every letter) by the Holy Spirit (Isaiah 30:8; 2 Timothy 3:16; Exodus 4:10-12). That verbal inspiration is extended equally and completely to every part of Scripture (plenary inspiration), and was delivered to faithful men who were specifically prepared by God to receive His revelation (2 Samuel 23:2; 2 Peter 1:20, 21). This was not a process of simple dictation, bur rather one of dual authorship in which the Holy Spirit so superintended the human authors that, through their individual personalities and different styles of writing, they composed and recorded God's word to man (2 Peter 1:20, 21), without error in the whole or in the part (Isaiah 30:8; 40:8; Matthew 5:18; 2 Timothy 3:16).

Grammatical Interpretation- Grammatical interpretation considers how words are used in discovering the meaning of a passage.

Historical Interpretation- Historical interpretation is understanding The Word in light of their historical context.

Inerrancy- Inerrancy is a term that means that the Scriptures possess the quality of freedom from error. They are exempt from the liability to mistake, incapable of error. In all their teachings they are in perfect accord with the truth.

Inscripturation- That supernatural process by which God caused men to write down the Divine revelation in the vocabularies and the styles of the human author, yet preserving complete accuracy in all that God intended to say (I Corinthians 2:12-13).

Inspiration- That quality, inherent in the autographs of Scripture, which render them just as much the Word of God as if God had personally breathed them out of His mouth (II Timothy 3:16).

Illumination- That special ability God gives people to understand the Scriptures to enable them to overcome specific areas of blindness. (John 16:13).

Interpretation- The discerning of the meaning of God's Word. For the purposes of this study a literal, historical grammatical interpretation will be employed (II Timothy 2:15).

Literal Interpretation- Literal interpretation is taking the words and sentences to mean what they would normally mean in the context in which they occur.

Preservation- By preservation of the Scriptures we mean that providential process by which God ensured that His word was passed down from generation to generation in a way that insured that it remained suitable for its intended purpose (John 10:35b).

Revelation- The supernatural impartation of truth, from God to man, of that which man could not otherwise know (I Corinthians 2:9-10).

Translation- Translation is to render into another language; to express the sense of in the words of another language; to interpret; hence, to explain or recapitulate in other words.

Revelation- The word *revelation* is derived from the Greek word *apokalupsis*, which means "disclosure" or "unveiling." Hence, revelation signifies God unveiling Himself to mankind. The fact that revelation has occurred renders theology possible; had God not revealed Himself there could be no accurate or propositional statements about God.[5]

Throughout the ages, man had gained knowledge through a variety of means. Though useful to the Lord for natural communication, these ordinary means were insufficient to communicate the dynamic truths of the Word of God. Therefore there was a need for a supernatural method for the impartation of truth from God to man, revelation.

Intuition is a natural internal confidence or belief, which comes from the disposition of the mind. An example is the ingrown knowledge of the existence of some sort of Supreme Being.

Empiricism is the method of discovery through one or more of the five senses. Sight, hearing, smell, taste and touch are limited to those physical things that can be learned in a natural manner.

Tradition is a system of learning that is passed down from person to person or group to group. There are truths that are learned in this manner however falsehood can just as easily be passed along in this manner. This poses a problem of

---

[5] Enns, Paul. *The Moody Handbook of Theology*. Chicago, Illinois: Moody Press, 1989.

determining what traditions may be trusted and which are simply "old wives tales." Additionally, tradition does not explain the sources of the information originally.

Reason is that judgment within man, which makes possible the pursuance of logical deductions based on those realities, which he observes. This method of discovery still requires the input of information.

In I Corinthians 2:9-10 we read:
> But as it is written: "Eye has not seen, nor ear heard, nor have entered into the heart of man the things which God has prepared for those who love Him." But God has revealed them to us through His Spirit. For the Spirit searches all things, yes, the deep things of God.

The Apostle Paul in explaining the impartation of information from God to man shows the inadequacies of the natural information gathering methods for this divine purpose. Though God can and has used the ordinary methods to communicate natural information, He developed a deeper technique of communication in order to convey the awesome truths of Scripture.

Paul wrote, "eye has not seen," a reference to the shortfall of empiricism for the discovery of the realities of God. Man cannot learn of the complexities of God through carnal methods.

He then said, "nor ear heard." This is a possible reference to the desire to learn of God through tradition. In Galatians 1:13 Paul told of his "former conduct in Judaism," and his persecution of "the church of God beyond measure" all due to his "being more exceedingly zealous for the traditions of my fathers." Paul understood that it was his zealousness for the traditions of his fathers that led to his sin against the church.

"Nor have entered into the heart of man." Not by empiricism nor by tradition nor even by reason or intuition does man learn of the deep things of God. "But God has revealed them to us through His Spirit. For the Spirit searches all things, yes, the deep things of God." This is revelation, the supernatural (outside of the confines of nature) impartation of truth, from God to man, of that which man could not otherwise know.

There are two types of revelation, Natural (or General) revelation and Special revelation. Natural Revelation is the revealing of God's existence using creation.

In Romans 1:18-20 we read (emphasis added):

> For the wrath of God is revealed from heaven against all ungodliness and unrighteousness of men, who suppress the truth in unrighteousness, because what may be known of God is manifest in them, **for God has shown *it* to them. For since the creation of the world His invisible *attributes* are clearly seen**, being understood by the things that are made, *even* His eternal power and Godhead, so that they are without excuse,

From the beginning of all time God has allowed His very creation to be a testimony of His existence. Though man has, within him, the knowledge of God he has "suppressed" it in unrighteousness, and is left without excuse.

Though testifying to the existence of God, Natural Revelation is not sufficient for salvation (Rom 10:17). In Psalm 19:1-6 we discover several points about Natural Revelation. First it is not bound by the confines of language. It is not communicated through speech. It is not heard in an audible manner nor is it bound by locale. Finally we see that it has not ceased but it is continuing.

In Acts Chapter 14, Paul and Silas were in the city of Lystra. While preaching the Gospel they were used of God to heal a man who had been crippled. The pagan people of the city, seeing this miraculous act, supposed that Paul and Silas were gods come down to walk among men. They began to bring livestock to sacrifice in their honor. Seeing this the Godly Apostle cried out, "Men, why are you doing these things? We also are men with the same nature as you, and preach to you that you should turn from these useless things to the living God, who made the heaven, the earth, the sea, and all things that are in them, who in bygone generations allowed all nations to walk in their own ways. **Nevertheless He did not leave Himself without witness, in that He did good, gave us rain from heaven and fruitful seasons,** filling our hearts with food and gladness (Acts 14:14-17)." God revealed to these men and to us His goodness and Divinity through His creation.

Special Revelation is the other type of Revelation. According to Paul Enns, Special Revelation is "the divine revealing of truth through Jesus Christ and through the Scriptures. In contrast to general revelation, which is available to everyone, special revelation is available only to those who have access to biblical truth."[6] The writer of Hebrews shows the revelation of Christ in Hebrews 1:1-2 (emphasis added):

> God, who at various times and in various ways spoke in time past to the fathers by the prophets, [2]**has in these last days spoken to us by *His* Son,** whom He has appointed heir of all things, through whom also He made the worlds;

Christ was the epitome of revelation during His incarnation here among His creation. His life was a demonstration to the very character of God the Father (John 14:9). The drawback is that though He was on the earth as a representation of the Godhead, He is no longer physically among us (Luke 24:6),

---

[6] Ibid

however He will again be available to those who believe (Acts 1:11).

The second form of Special Revelation is that of the Biblical Record. A first century fisherman named Peter speaks of the Biblical Revelation in 1 Peter 1:19-21:

> And so we have the prophetic word confirmed, which you do well to heed as a light that shines in a dark place, until the day dawns and the morning star rises in your hearts; knowing this first, that no prophecy of Scripture is of any private interpretation, for prophecy never came by the will of man, but holy men of God spoke *as they were* moved by the Holy Spirit.

Peter, a simple fisherman, a man recognized for having no formal education (Acts 4:13), explains the processes of revelation received by "Holy men of God."

Revealed to the original recipients and through them to us, the Word of God gives us first, the words of life, the Gospel of Christ, "the power of God unto Salvation" (Romans 1:16-17). Secondly, the very life skills needed to survive as a Christian in a hostile world are contained in the Holy Scriptures. In Psalm 19:7-11 we read:

> "The law of the LORD *is* perfect, converting the soul; The testimony of the LORD *is* sure, making wise the simple; The statutes of the LORD *are* right, rejoicing the heart; The commandment of the LORD *is* pure, enlightening the eyes; The fear of the LORD *is* clean, enduring forever; The judgments of the LORD *are* true *and* righteous together. More to be desired *are they* than gold, Yea, than much

fine gold; Sweeter also than honey and the honeycomb. Moreover by them Your servant is warned, *And* in keeping them *there is* great reward."

The same psalmist who demonstrated the Natural Revelation now tells of the written Word of God. First he tells of the soul saving power of the very Law of God. He then demonstrates the ability of the "testimonies of the lord to impart knowledge and wisdom to the simple. God's statutes and commandments make men's hearts celebrate and enlighten the eyes of men.

So what does the process of God's revelation to men of Biblical truths mean to us today? How does it relate? There are six main implications that one must consider to truly comprehend the true relationship between the Bible and revelation.

1. The Bible says in written words all that God had intended for us to know. "The secret *things belong* to the LORD our God, but those *things which are* revealed *belong* to us and to our children forever, that *we* may do all the words of this law (Deuteronomy 29:29).

2. Though all Scripture is given by inspiration of God, not everything recorded in Scripture is spoken by God. Men speak, Angels speak, Satan speaks and even animals speak (Genesis 3:1; 3:4-5; Numbers 22:28; Job 42:7).

3. Not everything within the Bible is truth. Everything in the Bible is accurate however, not everything in it is true. The Bible accurately records the lies of men and devils (Job 42:7; Gen 3:4-5).

4. Not everything revealed within the pages of Scripture is given for every person to do. As was said by Dr.

George Hare, "All Scripture is descriptive, but not all Scripture is prescriptive." An example of this truth is the four mutually exclusive diets given is Scripture that would be impossible to keep (Genesis 1:29; 9:1-4; Leviticus 11:1 Timothy 4:3-5).

5. Though the primary purpose of Scripture is to reveal God and His righteousness to man, not everything within Scripture is written for this purpose. Some of it is written for admonition (Now all these things happened to them as examples, and they were written for our admonition, upon whom the ends of the ages have come. 1 Corinthians 10:11). Other things were revealed for our learning (For whatever things were written before were written for our learning, that we through the patience and comfort of the Scriptures might have hope. Romans 15:4). Some Scripture was written for "doctrine, for reproof, for correction, for instruction in righteousness" 2 Timothy 3:16.

6. Not everything that is revelation to the readers of today was revelation to the human authors. Matthew's account of the life of Christ was not necessarily revelation to him; he lived it, felt the feelings, witnessed the events and suffered the consequences. It was not necessary to supernaturally reveal this information to him due to his experiencing it. That does not in any way effect the inspiration of his words. These things, though not revelation to the authors, are revelation to future readers. Only through the special revelation of God's word could we possibly have known of them.

In Hebrews 1:1-2 we read, "God, who at various times and in various ways spoke in time past to the fathers by the prophets, has in these last days spoken to us by *His* Son, whom He has appointed heir of all things, through whom also He made the worlds."

God has in times past communicated His word to men of God through various means. In many instances we see His use of "dreams" and "visions." In the *International Standard Bible Encyclopedia* we find this explained by Charles M. Stuart, M.A., D.D., Litt.D., LL.D., President Emeritus, Garrett Biblical Institute, Evanston, Illinois; La Jolla, California.

> Psychologists find that man is prevailingly and persistently "eye-minded." That is, in his waking life he is likely to think, imagine and remember in terms of vision. Naturally then, his dreaming is predominantly visual; so strongly visual, we are told, that it is not rare to find dreams defined as "trains of fantastic images." Whether man was made this way in order that God might communicate with him through dreams and visions is hardly worth debating; if the records of human life, in the Bible and out of it, are to be trusted at all, there is nothing better certified than that God has communicated with man in this way (Ps 89:19; Prov 29:18; compare Am 8:11,12; Hos 12:10). If one is disposed to regard the method as suited only to primitive peoples and superstitious natures, it still remains true that the experience is one associated with lives and characters of the most saintly and exalted kind (1 Sam 3:1; Jer 1:11; Ezek 1:1; Dan 2:19; Acts 9:10; 10:3; 16:9).
>
> The vision may come in one's waking moments (Dan 10:7; Acts 9:7); by day (Cornelius, Acts 10:3; Peter, Acts 10:9 ff; compare Nu 24:4,16) or night (Jacob, Gen 46:2); but commonly under conditions of dreaming (Nu 12:6; Job 4:13; Dan 4:9). The objects of vision, diverse and in some instances strange as they are, have usually their

points of contact with experiences of the daily life. Thus Isaiah's vision of the seraphim (Isa 6:2) was doubtless suggested by familiar figures used in the decoration of the temple at Jerusalem; Paul's "man of Macedonia" (Acts 16:9) had its origin in some poor helot whom Paul had seen on the streets of Troas and who embodied for him the pitiful misery of the regions across the sea; and "Jacob's ladder" (Gen 28:12) was but a fanciful development of the terraced land which he saw sun-glorified before him as he went to sleep. Among the recurring objects of vision are natural objects—rivers, mountains, trees, animals—with which man has daily and hourly association.

The character of the revelation through vision has a double aspect in the Biblical narrative. In one aspect it proposes a revelation for immediate direction, as in the ease of Abram (Gen 15:2 and frequently); Lot (Gen 19:15); Balaam (Nu 22:22), and Peter (Acts 12:7). In another aspect it deals with the development of the Kingdom of God as conditioned by the moral ideals of the people; such are the prophetic visions of Isaiah, Ezekiel, Hosea, and Micah, and the apocalypses of Daniel and John. The revelation for immediate direction has many correspondences in the life of the devout in all ages; the prophetic vision, dealing in a penetrating way with the sources of national growth and decay, has its nearest approach in the deliverances of publicists and statesmen who are persuaded that the laws of God, as expressed in self-control, truth, justice, and brotherly love, are supreme, and that the nations which disregard them are marked for ultimate and speedy extinction.

From the nature of the vision as an instrument of divine communication, the seeing of visions is naturally associated with revivals of religion (Ezek 12:21-25; Joel 2:28; compare Acts 2:17), and the absence of visions with spiritual decline (Isa 29:11,12; Lam 2:9; Ezek 7:26; Mic 3:6).

One may see visions without being visionary in the bad sense of that word. The outstanding characters to whom visions were vouchsafed in the history of Israel—Abraham, Moses, Jacob, David, Isaiah, Jesus and Paul—were all men of action as well as sentiment, and it is manifest from any fair reading of their lives that their work was helped and not hindered by this aspect of their fellowship with God. For always the vision emphasizes the play of a spiritual world; the response of a man's spirit to the appeal of that world; and the ordering of both worlds by an "intelligent and compelling Power able to communicate Himself to man and apparently supremely interested in the welfare of man.[7]

Another means that God chose was to communicate with man through verbal means. Though much more rare than dreams, visions and other methods, it is no less real. Moses, serving his father-in-law as a shepherd, encountered God's verbal communication at the famous burning bush (Exodus 3:4-14). God again communicated verbally with him in (Numbers 12:4).

---

[7] Orr James, *International Standard Bible Encyclopedia*: Cedar Rapids Parsons Technology, Inc.

We see examples of God's verbal communication in the lives of both Isaiah (Isaiah 6:8) and Samuel (1 Samuel 3:2-14).

God also communicated with saints of old through the inner communication of truth. In other words, God spoke to men and women not through verbal means, but through an inner voice. (Genesis 24:47-48; Exodus 15:24-25).

God also communicated with individual men through actual words written by God. Moses received the Ten Commandments from God's own "hand" (Exodus 34:1). In Daniel 5:1-6 we read (emphasis added),

> Belshazzar the king made a great feast for a thousand of his lords, and drank wine in the presence of the thousand. While he tasted the wine, Belshazzar gave the command to bring the gold and silver vessels, which his father Nebuchadnezzar had taken from the temple, which *had been* in Jerusalem, that the king and his lords, his wives, and his concubines might drink from them. Then they brought the gold vessels that had been taken from the temple of the house of God, which *had been* in Jerusalem; and the king and his lords, his wives, and his concubines drank from them. They drank wine, and praised the gods of gold and silver, bronze and iron, wood and stone. **In the same hour the fingers of a man's hand appeared and wrote opposite the lampstand on the plaster of the wall of the king's palace**; and the king saw the part of the hand that wrote. Then the king's countenance changed, and his thoughts troubled

him, so that the joints of his hips were loosened and his knees knocked against each other.

Belshazzar, the king of Babylon was the recipient of a direct written message from God.

Finally, God has communicated with man through christophanies (Old Testament appearances of Christ.) When we, in the English, read the phrase "the Angel of the Lord," it is safe to call that a preincarnate (before His birth) appearance of Jesus (Genesis 18:1; Judges 13:9; 17-18, 22).

Though in times past God communicated with believers in "diverse manners" today He has chosen to limit His communication to His written word. The revelation is complete. In other words God has revealed all that He intended to reveal and there is no necessity for further Revelation as of yet. He has told us how the story ends, and how to live a Godly life until that time. This inscripturated, inerrant, inspired written Word of God communicated God's truth through the experiences of the human authors (Exodus 15:22-24), their observances (Exodus 14:23,28), their thoughts (Psalm 51) and their research (Dan 9:2; Luke 4:1-4).

So what does all of this have to do with the Christian today? We are to use the available revelation of Scripture for the encouragement of the saints, "for doctrine, reproof, correction and instruction in righteousness" resulting in the completeness and equipping of the body of Christ.

Inerrancy
In the past it was sufficient to state that the Bible was inspired; however, it has now become necessary to define the evangelical position more precisely. The result, as Charles Ryrie has shown, has necessitated the inclusion of additional

verbiage. To state the orthodox view it is now necessary to include the terms "verbal, plenary, infallible, inerrant, unlimited inspiration![8]" All this has become necessary because of those who have claimed to believe words like *inspiration, infallible,* and even *inerrant* while denying that the Bible is free from error.

E. J. Young provides a suitable definition of inerrancy: "By this word we mean that the Scriptures possess the quality of freedom from error. They are exempt from the liability to mistake, incapable of error. In all their teachings they are in perfect accord with the truth[9]" Ryrie said, "God is true (Rom. 3:4); the Scriptures were breathed out by God (2 Tim. 3:16); therefore, the Scriptures are true (since they came from the breath of God who is true).[10]"

In defining inerrancy it is also important to state what it does not mean. It does not demand rigidity of style and verbatim quotations from the Old Testament. "The inerrancy of the Bible means simply that the Bible tells the truth. Truth can and does include approximations, free quotations, language of appearances, and different accounts of the same event as long as those do not contradict.[11]" At the Chicago meeting in October 1978, the International Council on Biblical Inerrancy issued the following statement on inerrancy: "Being wholly and verbally God-given, Scripture is without error or fault in all its teaching, no less in what it states about God's acts in creation, about the events of world history, and about its own literary origins under God, than in its witness to God's saving grace in individual lives.[12]"

---

[8] Charles C. Ryrie, *What You Should Know About Inerrancy,* Chicago, Illinois: Moody Press

[9] E. J. Young, *Thy Word Is Truth,* Carlisle, Pennsylvania: Banner of Truth

[10] Charles C. Ryrie, "Some Important Aspects of Biblical Inerrancy" *Bibliotheca Sacra* 136 (January-March, 1979):17.

[11] Charles C. Ryrie, *What You Should Know About Inerrancy,* Chicago, Illinois: Moody Press

[12] James Montgomery Boice, *Does Inerrancy Matter?* Oakland: International Council on Biblical Inerrancy

In a final definition it is noted that inerrancy extends to the original manuscripts: "Inerrancy means that when all the facts are known, the Scriptures in their original autographs and properly interpreted will be shown to be wholly true in everything they teach, whether that teaching has to do with doctrine, history, science, geography, geology, or other disciplines or knowledge.[13]"

To suggest there are errors in the Bible is to impugn the character of God. If the Bible has errors it is the same as suggesting that God can fail, that He can make a mistake. "To assume that God could speak a Word that was contrary to fact is to assume that God Himself cannot operate without error. The very nature of God is at stake.[14]"

Inscripturation
Inscripturation is that supernatural process by which God caused men to write down the Divine revelation in the vocabularies and the styles of the human author, yet preserving complete accuracy in all of that which God intended to say (I Corinthians 2:12-13).

Dr George Goolde has said, "as Christians we believe in a revealed religion." The Jewish religion is a faith that was revealed by God Himself, through the Scriptures and through His communication with the patriarchs. Christianity has its roots in that same revealed Judaism. Inscripturation is the method that God chose to give this "Revealed Religion" the objectivity required. It is the method that God chose to use to give us a standard that is outside of ourselves and is changeless, a true standard by which all other ideas, concepts or "revelations" must be measured. Revelation without an objective standard such as we have results in mysticism.

---

[13] IBID
[14] E. J. Young, *Thy Word Is Truth*, Carlisle, Pennsylvania: Banner of Truth

How do we understand Inscripturation as compared with revelation and inspiration? Revelation is the impartation of truth. The emphasis is on the content of the message. Inscripturation is the writing down the revelation. Here the emphasis on the process of writing and not the subject written. Inspiration is the quality inherent in the written product. When discussing inspiration, we see the emphasis is on the quality in distinction to the process.

As any other process, there is a method to Inscripturation. In the Apostle Paul's first letter to the Corinthians, he discusses this very process.

> Now we have received, not the spirit of the world, but the Spirit who is from God, that we might know the things that have been freely given to us by God. These things we also speak, not in words which man's wisdom teaches but which the Holy Spirit teaches, comparing spiritual things with spiritual [words].
>   -1 Corinthians 2:12-13

Paul is speaking of the Inscripturation that is allowed through the tutelage of the Holy Spirit. As with all things of the Spirit, Inscripturation originates with God Himself. Through the process of revelation the information is transferred to man (2 Samuel 23:1-3; Jeremiah 36:4, 17-18,23,27-32; 2 Peter 1:20-21). The authors were "taught by spirit [words]" comparing spiritual with spiritual. For example, Paul the apostle wrote much of the New Testament. The Holy Spirit compared the spiritual words in Paul's own vocabulary with the spiritual truth that God intended to communicate. This results in that concept that we call "Dual Authorship."

Inspiration

Inspiration is that quality, inherent in the autographs of Scripture, which render them just as much the Word of God as if God had personally breathed them out of His mouth.

> All Scripture [*Passe Graphe*] *is* given by inspiration of God [*Theopneustos*], and *is* profitable for doctrine, for reproof, for correction, for instruction in righteousness
> -II Timothy 3:16.

The Greek word *Theopneustos* is translated as "inspiration of God." A study of the word proves "God-breathed" a clearer understanding. Inspiration means that the Scriptures have the quality of God-breathedness. They are as much His word as if He had breathed them out of His mouth.

According to II Timothy 3:16 the *Graphe* (the thing written) is inspired. There is no Scripture that in any way leads us to say that the human authors were inspired. The authors were born, not God-breathed. In all of Scripture II Timothy 3:16 is the only place where *Theopneustos* is found. Therefore, the Scripture is the only thing inspired.

Some definitions by prominent evangelical theologians are as follows.

> Benjamin B. Warfield: "Inspiration is, therefore, usually defined as a supernatural influence exerted on the sacred writers by the Spirit of God, by virtue of which their writings are given Divine trustworthiness."[15]

---

[15] Enns, Paul. *The Moody Handbook of Theology*. Chicago, Illinois: Moody Press, 1989.

> Edward J. Young: "Inspiration is a superintendence of God the Holy Spirit over the writers of the Scriptures, as a result of which these Scriptures possess Divine authority and trustworthiness and, possessing such Divine authority and trustworthiness, are free from error."[16]

> Charles C. Ryrie: "Inspiration is . . . God's superintendence of the human authors so that, using their own individual personalities, they composed and recorded without error His revelation to man in the words of the original autographs."[17]

What is the extent of inspiration? *Passe Graphe,* "All the thing written." This extends to all of the words. We use the term "verbal plenary inspiration" to explain this.

Verbal inspiration- the very words are inspired not merely the concepts or ideas. Though the Holy Spirit inspired each and every word of Scripture He in no way superceded the individual personalities of the human authors. This is the concept of the Dual authorship of Scripture. Many scholars have stated that "the Bible IS not the Word of God however, it CONTAINS the Word of God." This is not sufficient. "All the thing written is God-breathed."

Plenary inspiration- the entire Bible is inspired. Not merely the words spoken by Christ. I heard a minister say, "You don't have to believe all of it (the Bible) but believe the red words."

Inspiration is necessary to preserve the revelation of God. If God has revealed Himself but the record of that revelation is

---

[16] IBID
[17] IBID

not accurately recorded, then the revelation of God is subject to question. Hence, inspiration guarantees the accuracy of the revelation.

Authority
Authority is the right, inherent in God and vested in Scripture, to demand response or obedience (James 1:22).

There is an Authority that is intrinsic within the Scriptures due to the fact of the inspiration. God lends to the Scriptures His own authority. In Romans 13:1 we read:

> Let every soul be subject to the governing authorities. For there is no authority except from God, and the authorities that exist are appointed by God.

According to Paul the Apostle, God is the source of all authority. "There is no authority except from God." There is a fundamental authority that only the Creator can lay claim to. Therefore, the word that He "breathes" carries with it that same authoritative quality.

How does today's Christian apply this authority? First the Scriptures hold authority to those original recipients. For instance the Law of Moses was given to the Israelites during a specific time. They were under the authority of that law. That authority does not now apply to New Testament believers. I as a believer in Christ Jesus am not required to keep the Levitical Diet or offer blood sacrifices to atone for my sins. However the revelation that was written to New Testament believers has the same authority over my life as the Law of Moses had over the Israelites. For instance I am to forgive another, even as God in Christ has forgiven me (Eph 4:32). There are two things that a believer is to do in reference to the Authority of Scripture.

1. One must interpret the command, learn its meaning. What was the purpose of the command? What were its specific requirements? Who was it given to?

2. Secondly, one must obey the commands that are applicable to the person's position in Christ. Considering Dispensations and ages one is to apply the command in measure to the relationship between you and the original recipients. If the original recipients were members of the Body of Christ and I am a member of the Body of Christ there is a full application of the authority of that Scripture. If the command was given to blasphemers and I too and a blasphemer then I must apply the command.

In addition to the authority of Scripture one should consider the sufficiency of Scripture. First we know that all Scripture is God-breathed. It has been given through a divine process and is therefore sufficient. However, it is also profitable (II Tim 3:16-17).

> All Scripture *is* given by inspiration of God, and *is* profitable for doctrine, for reproof, for correction, for instruction in righteousness, that the man of God may be complete, thoroughly equipped for every good work.

According to the Apostle, Scripture is sufficient to equip every believer for every good work. It is also sufficient to make every believer complete.

Animation
Animation is that element of life that is inherent in the Bible as in no other book (Hebrews 4:12).

Inanimate objects are incapable of self-function. A table, for instance, has no real ability to affect the lives of those who come into contact with it. Nor does a book in any real way. One can read an article from a major periodical, or a touching heart felt poem that can stir the emotions and even spur one on to some action or another. However, there is no book, no article or no poem that can touch much less save the human soul.

> For the Word of God *is* living and powerful, and sharper than any two-edged sword, piercing even to the division of soul and spirit, and of joints and marrow, and is a discerner of the thoughts and intents of the heart.
> –Hebrews 4:12

God has instilled within His word a quality of life. A quality of living power that can and does change lives. It is not some dead book with lifeless words lying powerless on dusty pages. It has power, the power to convict (II Timothy 3:16), the power to save souls (Romans 1:16-17; II Timothy 3:15; Psalm 19:7; I Peter 1:23), and the power to change lives by building faith (Romans 1:16).

The word has an ability to enhance the lives of believers in many ways. It "discerns the thoughts and intents of the heart" (Hebrews 4:12). It energizes life.

> "For this reason we also thank God without ceasing, because when you received the Word of God which you heard from us, you welcomed *it* not *as* the word of men, but as it is in truth, the Word of God, which also effectively works in you who believe." -I Thessalonians 2:13

It has the power to sanctify the believer (John 17:17). God's word guides the believer (Psalms 119:105). It causes growth

(Hebrews 5:12-13; I Peter 2:2; Acts 20:32), and it prevents sin (Psalm 119:11, Psalm 37:31).

John MacArthur said of the Word of God, "This book will keep you from sin and sin will keep you from this book."

Canonicity

Canonicity is the process of recognizing which books are intended by God to rule or measure our lives (Luke 24:44-45). A term used relative to the sixty-six books of the Bible, indicating they have passed the tests used to determine their inspiration and inclusion in the body of sacred Scripture.

Theologian, Dr. Paul Enns said of canonicity,

> "If the Scriptures are indeed inspired by God then a significant question arises: Which books are inspired? Historically, it was important for the people of God to determine which books God had inspired and which ones were recognized as authoritative.
>
> The word *canon* is used to describe the inspired books. The word comes from the Greek *kanon*... signifying a "measuring rod." The terms *canon* and *canonical* thus came to signify standards by which books were measured to determine whether or not they were inspired. It is important to note that religious councils at no time had any power to *cause* books to be inspired, rather they simply *recognized* that which God had inspired at the exact moment the books were written.

> Jews and conservative Christians alike have recognized the thirty-nine books of the Old Testament as inspired. Evangelical Protestants have recognized the twenty-seven books of the New Testament as inspired."

If one were to measure a box, the act of measuring does not constitute or even contribute to the actual mass of the object. Rather it merely describes the area already existing. In the same way, the process of canonization does not cause inspiration but simply recognizes the quality of inspiration already inherent with in the Word of God. Therefore, canonicity is based on inspiration; inspiration is not based on canonicity. The development of the canon is three fold. First, God inspired it. Next men of God recognized it. Finally, the people of God collected and preserved it.

The Men of God who recognized it, did so through a series of prerequisites. Geisler and Nix mention five principles in the discovering the canon:

1. Is it authoritative? Does it speak with authority?

2. Is it prophetic? Written by a man of God

3. Is it authentic? Tell the truth about God, man, sin

4. Is it dynamic? Does the book come with the power of God? The message of God will be backed by the might of God.

5. Was it received? Accepted by the people of God?[18]

---

[18] Geisler, Norman L.; William E. Nix *From God to Us*. Chicago, Illinois: Moody Press, 1974

Another testimony that we have to canonicity is from Christ himself. He quoted most of the 22 books of Hebrew canon. He considered every section (Law, Prophets, Writings) prophetic of him (Luke 24:27,44). Jesus Himself stated that the Old Testament was unbreakable (John 10:35). Additionally He mentioned individuals Jonah, Moses and Daniel. Jesus stated that the Scriptures were from God Himself (Matthew 15:3) and a product of the Holy Spirit (Mark 12:36). We even have silent testimony of Christ to the Scriptures through His submission to them (Matthew 4:1ff, Matthew 16:21-23). He taught the perpetuation of the Scriptures (Matthew 5:17-18, Matthew 24:35) as well as their supremacy over tradition (Mark 7:8-13). One final note, Christ quoted from even the Septuagint showing approval of even a translation of the Scriptures. This is interesting knowing that He had never quoted from any of the apocryphal books.

Illumination

Illumination is that special ability God gives people to understand the Scripture to enable them to overcome specific areas of blindness (John 16:13).

Oftentimes as a Christian is in study of God's word, he will experience a brilliant understanding that comes in a miraculous fashion. In attempting to explain this phenomenon he will often call it "revelation." The confusing of revelation with illumination is a common occurrence. Remember that revelation is the supernatural impartation of truth, from God to man, of that which man could not otherwise know. Illumination is that special ability given by God through the Holy Spirit to understand that which was already revealed.

The process of illumination is necessary for both the unsaved person as well as the saint. 1 Corinthians 1:18 says:

> For the message of the cross is foolishness to those who are perishing, but to us who are being saved it is the power of God.

Those who are without Christ cannot by nature, even because of nature, understand the complexities of the Word of God. Those who suffer from a "Christ deficiency" need the process of illumination to even comprehend the simplicities of the Gospel. Saints need the illumination of the Holy Spirit to discern the truths of God as revealed in Scripture.

As in most areas of theology, in the discussion of illumination the Trinity is front and center. Prior to Pentecost both the Father and the Son effected illumination.

Jesus asked a very pointed question of the disciples while in the area of Caesarea Philippi. Jesus asked His followers privately, "Who do men say that I, the Son of Man, am?" Peter the outspoken responded after some discussion, "You are the Christ, the Son of the living God." To this supernatural response Jesus replied, "Blessed are you, Simon Bar-Jonah, for flesh and blood has not revealed *this* to you, but My Father who is in heaven." Jesus knew that the Father illumined this truth to Peter (Matthew 16:13-17).

After Jesus had been crucified, two disciples were traveling from Jerusalem to Emmaus. Along the way Jesus, who they perceived as a stranger approached them. He asked them, "What kind of conversation *is* this that you have with one another as you walk and are sad?" At this point they spoke of the despair that they were experiencing at the death of the one whom they had hoped would be the savior of Israel. After spending some time with them, teaching them from the Scriptures, Jesus allowed them to recognize Him and departed from them. The men then said one to another, "did not our heart burn within us while He talked with us on the road, and while He opened the Scriptures to us" (Luke 24:13-32).

In the second chapter of Acts we see the gift given to all believers. From that time forward the Holy Spirit has taken up residence in the heart of every believer (Romans 12:1). This is significant in that we now, as believers, have the very author of Scripture living within us. While teaching the disciples in the upper room, Jesus revealed to them the plan of God to send the Holy Spirit to indwell all believers. He then describes the process of illumination.

> "Nevertheless I tell you the truth. It is to your advantage that I go away; for if I do not go away, the Helper will not come to you; but if I depart, I will send Him to you. And when He has come, He will convict the world of sin, and of righteousness, and of judgment: of sin, because they do not believe in Me; of righteousness, because I go to My Father and you see Me no more; of judgment, because the ruler of this world is judged. "I still have many things to say to you, but you cannot bear *them* now. However, when He, the Spirit of truth, has come, He will guide you into all truth; for He will not speak on His own *authority,* but whatever He hears He will speak; and He will tell you things to come."

Jesus said of the Holy Spirit, "when He, the Spirit of truth, has come, He will guide you into all truth." Who will guide the believer into truth? The Holy Spirit of God will guide the believer into truth. The Holy Spirit illumines the Word of God to the believer.

There is another area that Illumination impacts, that area of spiritual blindness. The chart bellow shows the relationship of Illumination and spiritual blindness.

Blindness	Subject of Blindness	Area of Blindness	God's Provision for Blindness	Scripture Reference
Natural	Unsaved	Perception of Revelation	Regeneration Renewed Mind	1 Cor 2:14 Titus 3:5
Satanic	Unsaved	Understanding of Salvation	Convicting Work of the Holy Spirit	2 Cor 4:3-4 John 16:7-11
Judicial	Israel	National Salvation	Future New Covenant with Israel	Rom 11:25 2 Cor 3:14-16 Jer 31:31-34
Carnal	Believers	Spiritual Discernment of Bible Truth for Growth	Teaching Ministry of the Holy Spirit	John 16:12-15 1Cor 3: 1-2 Heb 5:12-14 John 14:26 1 John 2:20-27

Interpretation

Interpretation is the discerning of the meaning of God's Word based on a literal grammatical and historical basis.

Who has the responsibility for interpreting the Bible? Is that not a duty of the clergy or the religious elite? The answer is a resounding no. For centuries the "laity" has been dissuaded from studying the Word of God for themselves. They have been told "that they were not trained to handle the oracles of God and thus they simply were not qualified. "The common man must not worry of such things, that is why the religious academics are here. We will tell you what you need to know." However the opposite is true. Paul the Apostle wrote to a young Christian and said, "Be diligent to present yourself approved to God, a worker who does not need to be ashamed, rightly dividing the word of truth" II Timothy 2:15.

It is the responsibility of each believer to interpret the Word of God for himself or herself. As for qualifications, the Holy Spirit of God who wrote the Scriptures dwells within you and illumines them for you. When the members of the body cease to read and interpret the Scriptures, when they cease to check after the teaching and preaching of those in the pulpits, when they take for granted what they are told, apostasy creeps in. The Charles Taze Russells[19] and the Joseph Smiths[20] begin to teach their false doctrines and their heresies go unnoticed by the sleeping multitudes.

Interpretation is important for other reasons. First, it has been said that revelation without interpretation produces mysticism. However, interpretation absent of revelation becomes rationalism.

Though we are commanded to interpret the Scriptures (II Timothy 2:15) and we state that it is the Holy Spirit who enables us to do that, we must still use wisdom and certain innate rules of interpretation. As has already been mentioned several times, the proper interpretive method employs a literal, grammatical, historical hermeneutic.

Literal Interpretation- Literal interpretation is taking the words and sentences to mean what they would normally mean in the context in which they occur.

David L. Cooper put it this way, "When the plain sense of Scripture makes common sense, seek no other sense." Many opponents of this method of interpretation (and yes there are those who do oppose it) accuse "literalists" of simplifying the Scriptures and ignoring the figurative literary methods used. This could not be more false. Those who employ a literal interpretation teach that when God uses figurative non-literal language, it is always clearly identified as figurative language. For a complete study on the subject of figures of speech see Bullinger's *Figures of Speech in the New Testament*.

Historical Interpretation Historical interpretation is the understanding of God's Word in light of its historical context.

---

[19] Founder of the Watchtower Bible and Tract Society (the Jehovah's Witnesses).
[20] Founder of the Church of Jesus Christ of Latter Day Saints (The Mormons).

Being mindful of historical implications of the text is a necessary part of a correct hermeneutical process. For instance, one must determine who the original recipients of the Scriptures were (e.g. Adam, Abraham, Israel, the Church, etc.). When was this particular instruction supposed to be carried out? Was this given during the dispensation of law or was it given in the church age. One must determine if there are any geographical areas or nations mentioned. Finally you must discover any cultural significance that may bear on the interpretation. For assistance in the cultural aspects of a specific passage see Ralph Gower's book, *The New Manners and Customs of Bible Times*.

Grammatical Interpretation Grammatical interpretation considers how words are used in discovering the meaning of a passage.

Just as expert carpenters must be thoroughly acquainted with the tools of their trade, so interpreters of Scripture must be with theirs. One must employ normal rules of grammar, taking into account parts of speech, number, tense, mood, case, and gender etc.

There are other things that must be considered in the science of Biblical interpretation. First, Scripture has only one right interpretation. We must never try to make the Bible say what we want it to say. We must first attempt to empty ourselves of our preconceptions and allow ourselves be molded by Scripture and not mold Scripture to our ideas. We cannot be afraid to say that we do not know. We also must never be afraid to state it when Scripture is silent regarding a particular subject. With this in mind, remember that there is only one right application for a given Scripture. The Bible is given for the purpose of increasing Godliness and not knowledge.

There are specific rules of interpretation that must be adhered to.

1. Scripture is the best interpreter of Scripture.

2. The interpreter must be guided by the Holy Spirit (John 16:13). Therefore the interpreter must be born again.

3. Interpret words in their context. Work from the larger context down to the immediate context.

4. Interpret predictive Scripture just as you would other Scripture.

5. Interpret less clear passages of Scripture in the light of more clear passages.

6. Do not assume any Scripture to be symbolic unless the passage claims to be.

7. Always ask the questions Who, What, When, Where, Why and How to discover the meaning of a passage.

Preservation
By preservation of the Scriptures we mean that providential process by which God ensured that His word was passed down from generation to generation in a way that insured that it remained suitable for its intended purpose.

Can the Scriptures ever be lost, or rendered unable to carry out their intended function? Jesus said to the Jews," The Scriptures cannot be broken" (John 10:35b). He also stated that not even the smallest letter would pass until all is fulfilled (Matthew 5:17-18). "Heaven and earth will pass away, but My words will by no means pass away" (Mark 13:31).

The preservation of the Scriptures took place through a process. The study of textual criticism, in which thousands of Biblical manuscripts are compared with the goal of determining what the autographs said, shows the preservation of the Scriptures. Though there are some noted differences in the copies that have been discovered, there is not one difference that changes the meaning or in any significant way dulls any area of doctrine! God has determined to communicate with mankind. He did so through revelation with the human authors of Scripture. He determined to facilitate the inscripturation or writing down of this revelation and He has preserved it to this very day.

Translation
Translation is to render into another language; to express the sense of in the words of another language; to interpret; hence, to explain or recapitulate in other words.

Each person from each ethnicity has his or her own "heart language." It is in this language that we learn the things that impact our lives. We can learn other languages and we can gain knowledge through this second language, but in order to really receive deep and abiding truths, we always turn to our heart language. With this in mind we understand that the Scriptures were written primarily in two ancient languages that most do not know. Therefore, there is a need for translating the Scriptures.

How does God look upon man's translating His word? Well, Jesus often quoted from a translation called the Septuagint. The Septuagint was a Greek translation of the Hebrew Scriptures. Commissioned about 125 years prior to Christ it was the popular version of the Scriptures in its day. Walter Martin said that the Septuagint was as common in the first century as the King James is today.

Conclusion
As we have discovered, God determined to communicate with mankind. Through the process of *revelation*, He communicated with the human authors. These men in turn *inscripturated* these *inspired* words. These autographs were brought together and *canonized* based on many criterion such as its *animation* and *authority*. Based on the need to communicate this Word of God

to a broader audience, he allowed us to *translate* it into the heart languages of the people while *preserving* it. He has given us this word and has charged us to study and *interpret* it for ourselves, which He assists us in through the process of *illumination*.

Eschatology
(The Doctrine of Last Things)

During the 1930's and 1940's, the London newspaper Sunday Express carried an astrology column by R. H. Naylor. Within a few weeks he predicted that Franco would never rule Spain, a united Ireland was imminent, and there would be no war in 1939. He explained that Hitler's horoscope showed he was not a war maker. So much for the horoscope! Today's astrologers do no better. On the rare occasions when their guesses are right, unthinking people tout them, never noticing the many, many times when they are wrong.[21]

---

[21] Robert C. Shannon, 1000 Windows, (Cincinnati, Ohio: Standard Publishing Company, 1997).

Prophecy is one of the great subjects of God's word. At least one-fifth of all Scripture was prophetic when it was written. That is, it announced things that would take place in the future. Much of that has now been fulfilled. What is left? That is the focus of this study. A study of the Last Things.

Labels
In a study there are many labels. One can be an Amillennialist, Postmillennialist, Premillennialists, Posttribulationalist, Pretribulationalist, Midtribulationalist or any number of other labels. I am going to take this time to defend the labels that fit me. I am a Premillennial Pretribulational rapturists.

The capstone to my theological perspective of eschatology is the imminent return of Christ. A careful observation of Prophetic Scripture would reveal that every Scripture that must be satisfied before Christ returns in the air to retrieve His saints has been fulfilled and there is no event in the way. Let us look at the coming events step by step. In doing so it is necessary to remember that all of the prophecies that have been fulfilled have been fulfilled in a literal sense. It then stands to reason that God in His immutable nature would fulfill the remaining prophecy in like manner.

STEP BY STEP

The Rapture:
The next event to occur is the rapture of the saints. Christ is going to return on the clouds to retrieve His saints.

> But I do not want you to be ignorant, brethren, concerning those who have fallen asleep, lest you sorrow as others who have no hope. For if we believe that Jesus died and rose again, even so God will bring with Him those who sleep in Jesus. For this we say to you by the word of the Lord, that we who are alive and remain until the coming of the Lord will by no means precede those who are asleep. For the Lord Himself will descend from heaven with a shout, with the voice of an archangel, and with the trumpet of God. And the dead in Christ will rise first. Then we who are alive and remain shall be caught up together with them in the clouds to meet the Lord in the air. And thus we shall always be with the Lord. Therefore comfort one another with these words.
>
> -1 Thessalonians 4:13-17

The words translated "Caught up together" are where we get the word "rapture." Rapture is the Latin translation of the Greek word used here. It is clear from this passage that Christ is not returning to rule and reign at this point. Look closely:

> For the Lord Himself will descend from heaven with a shout, with the voice of an archangel, and with the trumpet of God. And the dead in Christ will rise first. Then we who are alive and remain shall be caught up together with them in the clouds to meet the Lord in the air.

This Scripture does not refer to the triumphant warrior king found in Rev. 20:4. In stead it is the calling home of the saints. Look at the last part of that passage:

> And thus we shall always be with the Lord.

Just prior to the rapture, the tribulation period or the wrath of God takes place.

> For the wrath of God is revealed from heaven against all ungodliness and unrighteousness of men, who suppress the truth in unrighteousness,
> —Romans 1:18

> Therefore put to death your members, which are on the earth: fornication, uncleanness, passion, evil desire, and covetousness, which is idolatry. ⁶Because of these things the wrath of God is coming upon the sons of disobedience, in which you yourselves once walked when you lived in them.
> —Colossians 5:3-7

We know that the rapture occurs first because of many repeated promises that those who believe in the Son of God would be spared from the wrath of God.

> ...And to wait for His Son from heaven, whom He raised from the dead, even Jesus who delivers us from the wrath to come.
> —1 Thessalonians 1:10

> "Let not your heart be troubled; you believe in God, believe also in Me. In My Father's house

are many mansions; if it were not so, I would have told you. I go to prepare a place for you. And if I go and prepare a place for you, I will come again and receive you to Myself; that where I am, there you may be also. And where I go you know, and the way you know."

- John 14:1-3

Behold, I tell you a mystery: We shall not all sleep, but we shall all be changed—in a moment, in the twinkling of an eye, at the last trumpet. For the trumpet will sound, and the dead will be raised incorruptible, and we shall be changed. For this corruptible must put on incorruption, and this mortal must put on immortality. So when this corruptible has put on incorruption, and this mortal has put on immortality, then shall be brought to pass the saying that is written: "Death is swallowed up in victory." "O Death, where is your sting?   O Hades, where is your victory?" The sting of death is sin, and the strength of sin is the law. But thanks be to God, who gives us the victory through our Lord Jesus Christ.

-1 Corinthians 15:51-57

Once the rapture takes place that opens up the door for the appearance of the antichrist. This world leader will emerge on the scene and rocket to the top of the world political arena. He will make a covenant with Israel and then the temple will be rebuilt on the temple mount in Jerusalem. This time is well documented in Revelation 6-19.

The tribulation.

The Tribulation is the seventieth week of Daniel, a week according to the prophet's terminology equaling seven years. It is the last of a seventy-week (490 years) prophecy regarding Israel's future, which began in 444 B.C. Sixty-nine weeks (483 years) concluded with the death of Christ. See Daniel 9:24-27:

> "Seventy weeks are determined for your people and for your holy city, to finish the transgression, to make an end of sins, to make reconciliation for iniquity, to bring in everlasting righteousness, to seal up vision and prophecy, and to anoint the Most Holy. "Know therefore and understand, *that* from the going forth of the command to restore and build Jerusalem until Messiah the Prince, *there shall be* seven weeks and sixty-two weeks; the street shall be built again, and the wall, even in troublesome times. "And after the sixty-two weeks Messiah shall be cut off, but not for Himself; and the people of the prince who is to come shall destroy the city and the sanctuary. The end of it *shall be* with a flood, and till the end of the war desolations are determined. Then he shall confirm a covenant with many for one week; but in the middle of the week He shall bring an end to sacrifice and offering. And on the wing of abominations shall be one who makes desolate, even until the consummation, which is determined, is poured out on the desolate."

There is a gap between the sixty-ninth week and the seventieth week (the future Tribulation period). When Jesus taught about the events of the Tribulation in Matthew 24-25, He explained to the disciples what would happen to the *nation Israel*, indicating the Tribulation has reference to Israel.

The Tribulation will begin with the signing of the covenant by the antichrist, who promises to protect Israel.

> Then he shall confirm a covenant with many for one week; but in the middle of the week he shall bring an end to sacrifice and offering. And on the wing of abominations shall be one who makes desolate, even until the consummation, which is determined, Is poured out on the desolate."
>
> -Daniel 9:27

Technically, the rapture does not begin the Tribulation; there may be a brief period of time between the rapture of the church and the signing of the covenant.

The Tribulation will involve the judgment of God upon an unbelieving world. The tribulation is a time of wrath being poured out on the earth through a series of seals, trumpets, and bowl judgments. This period culminates with the triumphant return of Christ. (See. Rev. 19:11-21)

> Now I saw heaven opened, and behold, a white horse. And He who sat on him was called Faithful and True, and in righteousness He judges and makes war. His eyes were like a flame of fire, and on His head were many crowns. He had a name written that no one knew except Himself. He was clothed with a robe dipped in blood, and His name is called The Word of God. And the armies in heaven, clothed in fine linen, white and clean, followed Him on white horses. Now out of His mouth

goes a sharp sword, that with it He should strike the nations. And He Himself will rule them with a rod of iron. He Himself treads the winepress of the fierceness and wrath of Almighty God. And He has on His robe and on His thigh a name written:

KING OF KINGS AND LORD OF LORDS.

Then I saw an angel standing in the sun; and he cried with a loud voice, saying to all the birds that fly in the midst of heaven, "Come and gather together for the supper of the great God, that you may eat the flesh of kings, the flesh of captains, the flesh of mighty men, the flesh of horses and of those who sit on them, and the flesh of all people, free and slave, both small and great." And I saw the beast, the kings of the earth, and their armies, gathered together to make war against Him who sat on the horse and against His army. Then the beast was captured, and with him the false prophet who worked signs in his presence, by which he deceived those who received the mark of the beast and those who worshiped his image. These two were cast alive into the lake of fire burning with brimstone. And the rest were killed with the sword which proceeded from the mouth of Him who sat on the horse. And all the birds were filled with their flesh.

The tribulation period is divided into two periods. The tribulation and the Great Tribulation.

> For then there will be great tribulation, such as has not been since the beginning of the world until this time, no, nor ever shall be.
> –Matthew 24:21

Why does there need to be such a time? The first reason of the Tribulation is to cause the conversion of Israel, which will be accomplished through God's disciplinary dealing with Israel. The second purpose of the Tribulation is to judge unbelieving people and nations.

Judgment seat of Christ.

The judgment seat of Christ is mentioned in Romans 14:10, 1 Corinthians 3:9-15, and 2 Corinthians 5:10. It does not indicate a judgment concerning eternal destiny but instead a place of reward for Christians for faithfulness. The purpose of the judgment seat will be to reward Christians for their service.

> For we must all appear before the judgment seat of Christ, that each one may receive the things done in the body, according to what he has done, whether good or bad.
> –2 Corinthians 5:10

That the rewarding takes place prior to the Second Advent is seen in that the bride has already been rewarded when returning with Christ.

Marriage of the Lamb.

Before the Second Coming of Christ, the marriage takes place in heaven. The marriage has to do with the church and takes place in heaven. The marriage supper has to do with Israel and takes place on earth in the form of the millennial kingdom.

Second coming of Christ.

At the end of the Tribulation Christ will return physically to earth to render judgment and to inaugurate the millennial kingdom.

> When the Son of Man comes in His glory, and all the holy angels with Him, then He will sit on the throne of His glory.
>
> - Matthew 25:31

> And I saw thrones, and they sat on them, and judgment was committed to them. Then I saw the souls of those who had been beheaded for their witness to Jesus and for the Word of God, who had not worshiped the beast or his image, and had not received his mark on their foreheads or on their hands. And they lived and reigned with Christ for a thousand years.
>
> -Revelation 20:4

The Old Testament and Tribulation saints will be raised at that time to inherit the kingdom. At the Second Coming Christ will judge Jews and Gentiles. The Jews will be judged on the basis of their preparedness for His return and their faithfulness as stewards of the Word of God. The saved Jews will enter the millennial kingdom.

> His lord said to him, 'Well done, good and faithful servant; you were faithful over a few things, I will make you ruler over many things. Enter into the joy of your lord.'
>
> -Matt. 25:21

Meanwhile the unsaved will be cast into outer darkness.

Millennial kingdom.

When Christ returns to earth He will establish Himself as King in Jerusalem, sitting on the throne of David.

> He will be great, and will be called the Son of the Highest; and the Lord God will give Him the throne of His father David. And He will reign over the house of Jacob forever, and of His kingdom there will be no end."
>
> -Luke 1:32-33

At the Second Advent the covenants of Israel will be fulfilled as Israel is regathered from the nations and restored to the land under the Messiah.

The conditions during the Millennium will depict a perfect environment physically and spiritually. It will be a time of peace, joy, comfort, and no poverty or sickness. Because only the believers will enter the Millennium, it will be a time of righteousness, obedience, holiness, truth and fullness of the Holy Spirit. Christ will rule as king, with David as regent, nobles and governors will also rule.

At the end of the Millennium the unsaved dead of all ages are resurrected and judged at the great white throne. They will be condemned and cast into the lake of fire, their final abode.

> Then I saw a great white throne and Him who sat on it, from whose face the earth and the heaven fled away. And there was found no place for them. And I saw the dead, small and great, standing before God, and books were opened. And another book was opened, which is the Book of Life. And the dead were judged according to their works, by the things, which

> were written in the books. The sea gave up the dead who were in it, and Death and Hades delivered up the dead who were in them. And they were judged, each one according to his works. Then Death and Hades were cast into the lake of fire. This is the second death. And anyone not found written in the Book of Life was cast into the lake of fire.
> - Rev. 20:11-15

The devil, the Antichrist, and the false prophet are also cast into the lake of fire.

> The devil, who deceived them, was cast into the lake of fire and brimstone where the beast and the false prophet are. And they will be tormented day and night forever and ever.
> - Rev. 20:10

Eternal state.
Following the Millennium, the heavens and the earth are judged, because they were the province of Satan's rebellion against God. The eternal state, the abode of all redeemed, will be ushered in as seen in Revelation 21-22.

Hamartiology
(The Doctrine of Sin)

Western culture has made a fundamental change in its religious base. We have exchanged that One who said, "I am the Truth" for the incredibly expensive doctrine of Freud and the words of all his varied disciples. Our new religion says with Pontius Pilate, "What is truth?" and teaches that our status is one of "original victim" rather than "original Sin."

Sin is... This has been the discussion of the ages. Sin is "missing the mark." Sin is a debt, or a void. Sin is knowingly violating the law of God. Oswald Chambers said, "The essence of sin is the refusal to recognize that we are accountable to God at all. " Sin is all of that and it is more.

Rather than dwelling on an attempt of defining sin any more than above I hope to examine the effects of sin on mankind. Searching the relationship of sin as to the nature of man.

The nature of man

Philosophy and psychology have their explanations for man. Philosophy says that man is essentially good. That he is inherently good. Psychology adds the factors of heredity and environment as excuses for mankind. Naturalistic theories have always held to the natural goodness of man. Even theological forms may imply that man can assist in his own salvation because of the spark of good within us all. Any excuse to disregard God is taken. There is a do-it-yourself attitude out there that says that if we can just get hold of our selves we can change for the better. Men are always seeking "self-improvement." They are trying to go to hell with a positive mental attitude. Christian Science says that human nature is totally good.[22] What you think is bad is not bad. One big difference between Christian Science and evangelical Christianity is this: They look at mankind and they say that bad is not really bad, that bad does not exist. We answer them by saying, The good that you see is not really there.

In this day, a great many Christians are going to psychiatrists, thinking that they can solve their problems. They cannot. Fundamentally they are missing what the Word of God has to say. The Scriptures tell us that the human family is totally

---

[22] Brooks, Keith L., *The Spirit of Truth and the Spirit of Error* (Chicago: Moody Press, 1985).

depraved. The Bible says there was a fall, and in the third chapter of Genesis we see it:

> Now the serpent was more cunning than any beast of the field, which the LORD God had made. And he said to the woman, "Has God indeed said, 'You shall not eat of every tree of the garden'?" And the woman said to the serpent, "We may eat the fruit of the trees of the garden; but of the fruit of the tree which is in the midst of the garden, God has said, 'you shall not eat it, nor shall you touch it, lest you die.'"

> Then the serpent said to the woman, "You will not surely die. For God knows that in the day you eat of it your eyes will be opened, and you will be like God, knowing good and evil." So when the woman saw that the tree was good for food, that it was pleasant to the eyes, and a tree desirable to make one wise, she took of its fruit and ate. She also gave to her husband with her, and he ate.

That was the fall. Look in Romans Five for the result:

> Therefore, just as through one man sin entered the world, and death through sin, and thus death spread to all men, because all sinned.
> —Romans 5:12

When Paul says, "all men have sinned," he does not mean that they have committed individual acts of sin, though they have. He means that in Adam they sinned; that is, what Adam did they did. Adam's sin was imputed or given over to us as his human family. Back in the Garden of Eden Adam sinned against God. When he did that he plunged all who came from him into sin. The result of the fall is that man has been brought to the place of death. That, after all, is the proof. By man came death. In Adam all die. We are tied to Adam whether we like it or not. This is the reason a little infant dies who has no committed sin of his own. He has Adam's.

Three pieces of Evidence

1. Historical Proof

History itself is proof of the fallen nature of man, of his total and complete depravity. A simple look at society reveals it.

> Art is a reflection of a society's most profound aspirations. Cultures exalt their highest ideals. In the middle Ages, it was the divine. For the 18th and 19th centuries, it was Man as Promethean hero. Today, it's the depraved, life as a freak show. Our cultural mavens wallow in the sordid, celebrate the nauseating, and dwell on their imaginary persecution.[23]

Look at the depraved attitude of so called "world leaders." Hitler, Mussolini, Lennon and Castro. Look at the downslide of society even now. There is no sane man who can look at society, nod his head in satisfaction and exclaim, "Yes, it is getting much better."

2. The Conscience of Man

In an article called *Guilt*, psychologist William James wrote,

> "One single word which torments more Americans in more unexpected ways than any

---

[23] Feder, Don, The *Boston Herald* (July 27, 1993). Christianity Today, Vol. 41, no. 8.

> other disease of the mind or body, one word, guilt."

Guilt is that one thing that the psychologist is probing for. He starts looking for that tender spot that hidden memory that is causing the guilty feeling.

In Romans 2 we learn something about ourselves:
> For as many as have sinned without law will also perish without law, and as many as have sinned in the law will be judged by the law (for not the hearers of the law are just in the sight of God, but the doers of the law will be justified; for when Gentiles, who do not have the law, by nature do the things in the law, these, although not having the law, are a law to themselves, who show the work of the law written in their hearts, their **conscience** also bearing witness, and between themselves their thoughts accusing or else excusing them) in the day when God will judge the secrets of men by Jesus Christ, according to my Gospel.
> –Romans 2:12-16

Even though the Gentiles were not familiar with God's law, they still knew that lying, stealing and murder were wrong. Their consciences were used by God to point out their evil.

The good news is that Christ does not leave us in that guilt. Romans 8:1 relieves us of this horrible condition:

> There is therefore now no condemnation to those who are in Christ Jesus, who do not walk according to the flesh, but according to the Spirit.

By nature we are guilty. But in our new nature, in Christ we are free from that guilt, our sins are removed from us "as far as the east is from the west."

3. THE WORD OF GOD

The final piece of evidence in this trial against mankind is the very Word of God.

> for all have sinned and fall short of the glory of God,
>
> -Romans 3:23

David the King of Israel, the man who was called the "Apple of God's eye," said this:

> For I acknowledge my transgressions, and my sin is always before me. Against You, You only, have I sinned, and done this evil in Your sight— That You may be found just when You speak, and blameless when You judge. **Behold, I was brought forth in iniquity, and in sin my mother conceived me.**
>
> —Psalm 51:3-5

In other words, David understood that he started off in sin. He knew that he had a sinful nature and he was born to it. Job knew it:

> Who can bring a clean thing out of an unclean? No one!
>
> -Job 14:4

Jesus told Nicodemus how to be saved:
> "Most assuredly, I say to you, unless one is born again, he cannot see the kingdom of God."

> Nicodemus said to Him, "How can a man be born when he is old? Can he enter a second time into his mother's womb and be born?" Jesus answered, "Most assuredly, I say to you, unless one is born of water and the Spirit, he cannot enter the kingdom of God. **That which is born of the flesh is flesh**, and that which is born of the Spirit is spirit.
>
> –John 3:3-6

Flesh will always be flesh, it's nothing but flesh and we cannot change it. Even God does not change the nature of the flesh; He instead gives us a new nature. You must be born again; the old nature is not even going to be salvaged.

Concerning this old flesh, God admonishes us to "put off… your former conduct, the old man which grows corrupt according to the deceitful lusts." -Ephesians 4:22. Look at these other Scriptures.

> And you, who once were alienated and enemies in your mind by wicked works, yet now He has reconciled.
>
> --Colossians 1:21

> "The heart is deceitful above all things, and desperately wicked; Who can know it?
>
> --Jeremiah 17:9

> Indeed, You have made my days as handbreadths, and my age is as nothing before You; certainly every man at his best state is but vapor.
>
> –Psalm 39:5

Even when you are at your best, you are only a vapor from vanity. C.S. Lewis said, "No man knows how bad he is until he has tried very hard to be good.[24]" Notice what the Lord has to say concerning this:

> If you then, being evil, know how to give good gifts to your children, how much more will your heavenly Father give the Holy Spirit to those who ask Him!"
>
> --Luke 11:13

Look again to the psalmist:

> They have all turned aside, they have together become corrupt; There is none who does good, no, not one.
>
> –Psalm 14:5

What a tremendous response by Jesus when the adulterous woman was thrown at His feet. The religious elite battered Him for a response to their question of what should be her fate. "So when they continued asking Him, He raised Himself up and said to them, 'He who is without sin among you, let him throw a stone at her first'" (John 8:7). Dr. G. Campbell Morgan remarked, "That took me out of the stone-throwing business,[25]" and it should take us all out of it.

---

[24] Lewis, C.S., *The Quotable Lewis*, (Wheaton: Tyndale, 1989).
[25] Morgan, G. Campbell, *The Best of G. Campbell Morgan* (from The Westminster Booklets). Christianity Today, Vol. 35, no. 3.

Anthropology
(The Doctrine of Man)

MAN'S FIXATION ON HIS ORIGINS
"Night owls may become bedbugs on Sunday morning, but this does not prove evolution[26]." Man has speculated concerning his origins from the very beginning. Due to man's constant interest in himself, and yes, his egocentric nature he has made his own origins of great interest. The study of man's origins has ranged from the plausible to the very surreal. An example of the worst sort is from recent thought. There is a group called the Onanokees. They are of the belief that there is a planet called Onanokee that passes through our Solar System every twenty six thousand years. During its last pass their atmosphere was dying. The only hope of saving their planet was to mine

---

[26] Pentz, Croft M., *The Complete Book of Zingers* (Wheaton: Tyndale House Publishers, Inc., 1990)

the gold of Earth to purify their atmosphere. While a small landing party was on earth, extracting the life saving gold, their home planet orbited out of range and they were stranded here. This is, they teach, the origin of man.

THE TWO MOST ACCEPTED EXPLANATIONS
Though there are many theories that encompass the thinking of most concerning the origins on man, here we are only going to examine two. First we will look at the theory of Evolution. We will explore briefly what the evolutionist believes and why. We will then look at the Biblical account of Creation, showing how the Biblical account fills in the gaps that are left in the Evolutionary model.

NATURALISTIC EVOLUTION
The first thing that I must impress upon the reader is that Naturalistic or Biological Evolution leaves no room for God. Frank Peretti in his lecture called "the Chair[27]" sums up the theory of evolution as "From goo to you by way of the zoo."

The one thing that characterizes evolution is its godlessness, which accounts for its popularity. It has afforded man an explanation for the origin of man without having to acknowledge God. It has, in fact, gained such popularity that is it almost exclusively taught in our public schools. It is not taught as theory but as fact. Many believe that all scientists were atheistic, however that is far from the truth. Larry Vardiman of the Institute for Creation Research wrote of Sir Isaac Newton,

> Isaac Newton is recognized today by almost all scientists to have been one of the greatest, if not the greatest, scientist who ever lived. His breadth of knowledge, his ability to analyze and synthesize the physical world, his development

---
[27] Peretti, Frank, *The Chair* (Coeur d'Alene, Id Compass international, 1997)

and use of the calculus, his formulation of the three laws of motion, and the expression of the law of gravitation have been unequaled by any other scientist before or since.

Yet, it is not widely known that Newton was also a Christian and a Bible scholar. He studied the Bible diligently and wrote commentaries on portions of Scripture, such as his monograph on the book of Daniel. He clearly believed that God is the Creator and sustainer of our universe. Misunderstanding the source of Newton's creativity, some critics have suggested that Newton would have been more productive if he had not wasted so much time studying and writing about the Bible[28].

There are three main areas of difficulty that the evolutionist must face.

1. From nothing to the inorganic
2. From the inorganic to the organic
3. From the organic to man

Let us carefully look at each of these areas.

FROM NOTHING TO THE INORGANIC
In other words, where did matter come from? Science today is unable to explain from nothing to the inorganic. There is no

---

[28] Vardiman, Larry, "Newton's Approach to Science: Honoring Scripture" (Santee Ca. ICR 1997)

explanation. Recently we have learned that the universe is much vaster than we had ever thought and I believe that it is greater yet than we may realize. And despite our best efforts, our searching this earth, our own solar system and even attempting to look and listen to the deepest space, we have not been able to explain from nothing to the inorganic. It is one thing to say that a single cell developed and eventually became a man over a long expanse of time. But one must be able to say where the single cell came from. How did it all begin? You must be able to go back into time someplace and tell how it all came into existence.

The truth be known, there is only one explanation that can satisfactorily reveal the origin of matter. "In the beginning God created the heavens and earth." Gen 1:1. That is the only logical explanation that there can be. Evolution has no explanation nor can they even begin to come up with an attempt.

FROM INORGANIC TO THE ORGANIC
The next area of difficulty for the evolutionist is going from the inorganic to the organic. No one in any area of science has been able to bridge this chasm. No area of study nor experimentation has been able to explain how life began. What is behind it? How can that which is inorganic, live? Science has spared no expense in this area of study. Many of the brightest minds of the scientific community have invested years of their lives and billions of dollars and they are no closer to explaining life than they were a thousand years ago. Dr. J. Vernon McGee wrote on this subject and he said,

> "Just to push our thinking out there in the ocean and claim our ancestors came from seaweed millions of years ago doesn't answer anything at

all. If you want to know the truth, no theory has solved the problem.[29]"

FROM ORGANIC TO MAN

Finally there is the third step, going from the organic to man. Dr. Duane T. Gish of the ICR wrote,

> According to a mechanistic, naturalistic view of the universe, and thus of origins, the whole of reality is evolution — a single process of self-transformation. Everything in the universe, according to this view, has evolved from a primordial chaotic or random state of matter. This evolutionary continuum thus requires that life arose on this planet (or on some planet, at least) from inanimate matter via chemical and physical processes still operating today. It is generally believed that these processes acted for many tens of millions of years, most likely hundreds of millions of years, before true cellular life was brought into being.

> The first thing that may be said about theories on the origin of life is that none satisfy the criteria of a scientific theory. There were no human observers of the origin of life, and it is impossible to reenact the process. If such a process did occur, it could have left no fossil record or history[30].

---

[29] McGee, J. Vernon, *Doctrine for difficult days* (Nashville: Thomas Nelson Publishers, 1996)
[30] Gish, Duane, *Vital Articles on Science/Creation* (Santee Ca. ICR 1997)

Even evolutionists have acknowledged the lack of scientific procedure in the attempt to explain God out of the origin of man debate. Dr. J.D. Bernal, in a discussion of a paper by Dr. Mora, a prominent evolutionist, wrote,

> " ... Dr. Mora has shown that the principles of experimental science do not apply to discussions on the origin of life, and indeed cannot apply to any problem of origin.[31] "

God created the whales, the fish and the animal kingdom but man is a separate creation. Evolutionists have never been able to bridge the tremendous gap between the inorganic dust of the earth to man. There is no natural transition from inorganic dust to animals nor from animals to man and any attempt to prove that one exists is quickly disproved. Remember Piltdown man? The evolutionist hopes were pinned on this "man" from Great Britain. He was proved to be a forgery.

Science in their advancement of Evolution has failed to answer any of these questions. They cannot tell you how nothing became lifeless matter. They cannot tell you how this lifeless matter became full of life. And they cannot tell you how life became man. Even some evolutionist have resigned themselves to the knowledge that their "science" was based on faith more than science,

> "My attempts to demonstrate evolution by experiment carried on for more than forty years have completely failed... At least I should

---

[31] Bernal, J. D., in *The Origins of Prebiological Systems and of Their Molecular Matrices*, (Ed. S. W. Fox, Academic Press, New York, 1965)

> hardly be accused of having started from a preconceived anti-evolutionary standpoint... It may be firmly maintained that it is not even possible to make a caricature out of paleobiological facts. The fossil material is so complete that it has been possible to construct new classes, and the lack of transitional series cannot be explained as due to the scarcity of material. Deficiencies are real. They will never be filled... The idea of an evolution rests on pure belief.[32]"
>
> –Dr. Heribert Nilsson

Dr. Nilsson has moved from science and into religion. To be an evolutionist you must take it by faith. Evolution is and has been the official religion of the Humanists.

BIBLICAL CREATIONISM

Once one determines to reject evolution he is left with few choices. Other than way-out theories that involve alien invasion and other such nonsense we are left with the truth of Biblical Creationism. Of all of the questions that we asked about evolution, it is Biblical Creationism that answers not one but all three of them.

FROM NOTHING TO THE INORGANIC

> In the beginning God created the heavens and the earth. The earth was without form, and void; and darkness *was* on the face of the deep. And

---

[32] Nilsson, Heribert, *Synthetic Artbuilding*, *Vols 1-2* (Lund, Sweden: Velaq Cuk Gleerup, 1953)

> the Spirit of God was hovering over the face of the waters.
>
> -Genesis 1:1-2

God created. That is the answer for those who would ask how the nothing became the inorganic. God created. Sir Isaac Newton, the hero of all scientists, concerning God's creation said this,

> This most beautiful system of the sun, planets, and comets, could only proceed from the counsel and dominion of an intelligent and powerful Being. This Being governs all things, not as the soul of the world, but as Lord over all; and on account of his dominion he is wont to be called Lord God.[33]

In the beginning God created the heaven and the earth. He then created Light. This was in the first day of creation. All of which is the inorganic. Notice that there is yet no life created.

On the second day, God said, "Let there be a firmament in the midst of the waters, and let it divide the waters from the waters" Gen 1:6. This is the canopy that enveloped the earth. This canopy of water protected the earth from the rays from the sun. This is part of the answer to the famous question, "Explain the longetivity of the antediluvians."

FROM THE INORGANIC TO THE ORGANIC

It was on the third day of creation that God answered the second question. After arranging the lands and water He said, "Let the earth bring forth grass, the herb *that* yields seed, *and*

---

[33] Newton, Isaac, *Christian History, no. 30*, "Women in the Medieval Church" (Reprint Oregon Institute of Science & Medicine 1991)

the fruit tree *that* yields fruit according to its kind, whose seed *is* in itself, on the earth"; and it was so" Gen 1:11. There was no cosmic accident that resulted in life, there was no electrification of dust and sludge that resulted in the first life, God simply spoke it into existence. The evolutionist will retort, "You cannot prove these wild speculations." But neither can he prove or disprove God's. In fact the harder one tries to prove God a farce the closer he comes to proving God as creator.

On the fourth day God returned to the inorganic. He created the sun the moon and all of the stars. These new plants and trees would need light and God supplied.

On day five God moved far beyond all that he had done yet. It was this day that he created the "great sea creatures and every living thing that moves, with which the waters abounded, according to their kind, and every winged bird according to its kind. And God saw that *it was* good" Gen 1:21.

FROM THE ORGANIC TO MAN

It was Day six that God completed His masterpiece. As wonderful the creation of the inorganic from nothing was, as great as the creation of the birds of the air and creatures of the sea were they paled in comparison to the creation of man. Man was created in the image of God, for the purposes of fellowship with Him. This was the grand idea the reason for all that had been done God's magnum opus. What is it that makes man so special among all of God's creatures? Victor Hugo answers it this way,

> There is one spectacle greater than the sea: That is the sky; there is one spectacle greater than the sky: That is the interior of the soul[34].

---

[34] Hugo, Victor *Victor Hugo in Les Miserables.* Christianity Today, Vol. 37, no. 6.

What separates man from all other creatures under the sun? Is it personality, will, intelligence? No. It is simply that indefinable quality that ties us to God it is the soul. What is it that absolutely disproves any type of evolution? What is it that demands that we reject Biological Evolution, Theistic Evolution Progressive Creationism or any other answer other than Biblical Creationism? The Soul. William Jennings Bryan said,

> What shall we say of the intelligence of those who distinguish between fishes and reptiles and birds, but put a man with an immortal soul in the same circle with the wolf, the hyena, and the skunk? There is no more reason to believe that man descended from an inferior animal than there is to believe that a stately mansion has descended from a small cottage[35].

The Humanist has hijacked the educational system. He has imposed upon our youth and young adults his religion. Evolution is the atheist's way of banning God from His creation. It is their way of suppressing what may be known of God (Rom 1:19).

> It shall be unlawful for any teacher in any of the universities, normals, and all other public schools of the State which are supported in whole or in part by the public school funds of the State, to teach any theory that denies the story of the divine creation of man as taught in the Bible, and to teach instead that man has descended from a lower order of animals[36].

---

[35] Draper, Edythe, *Draper's Book of Quotations for the Christian World*. (Wheaton, Tyndale House Publishers, 1992)
[36] Tennessee Legislature Act, March 21, 1925. Repealed, May 17, 1967

Angelology
(The Doctrine of Angels)

Have you ever seen an angel? John G. Paton believes he has. While he was a missionary in the New Hebrides Islands, hostile natives surrounded his mission headquarters one night, intent on burning the Patons out and killing them. Paton and his wife prayed all that night. At dawn they were amazed to see the attackers just turn and leave. A year later the chief of that very tribe was converted to Christianity. Paton then asked him what had kept him and his men from burning down the house and killing them that night. The chief asked Paton a return question: "Who were all those men you had with you there?" Paton told him there had been no one except his wife and himself, but the chief insisted they had seen hundreds of men standing guard--big men in shining garments with drawn swords.

First we need to acknowledge something. All that we can sense with our five senses does not constitute all that exists. We need to recognize that creation is not limited to our sense perception. It's not limited to what we can see or feel or what is tangible.

There is only one reliable place to gain the information that we are seeking. The word of God contains the only dependable information concerning angels.

WHAT ARE ANGELS?

The Greek word for angel is *angelos*, which means messenger. It sometimes refers to men, men's spirits and to created beings who serve as God's messengers. The word occurs 108 times in the Old Testament and 165 times in the New Testament. So we can see that the Bible has quite a lot to say about them.

Angels are a creation of God
Angels are created beings. In Nehemiah 9:6 says,

> You alone are the LORD; You have made heaven, the heaven of heavens, with all their host, the earth and everything on it, the seas and all that is in them, and You preserve them all. The host of heaven worships You.

Nehemiah wrote that the "host" of heaven were among God's creation. In Colossians we read of this process of creation,

> For by Him all things were created that are in heaven and that are on earth, visible and invisible, whether thrones or dominions or principalities or powers. All things were created through Him and for Him. And He is before all things, and in Him all things consist.
> —Colossians 1:16-17

Christ is praised as the creator of all things. There is nothing created that was not created through Him. This includes the angels. I was once studying the gospel account of the demon Legion.

> Then they sailed to the country of the Gadarenes, which is opposite Galilee. And when He stepped out on the land, there met Him a certain man... When he saw Jesus, he cried out,

> fell down before Him, and with a loud voice said, "What have I to do with You, Jesus, Son of the Most High God? I beg You, do not torment me!" For He had commanded the unclean spirit to come out of the man. Jesus asked him, saying, "What is your name?" And he said, "Legion," because many demons had entered him.
>
> –Luke 8:26-30

Two things in this account intrigued me. The first of which was that the demon recognized Jesus for who He really was, the Son of the Most High. Of course they did, He had created them as beautiful angelic beings and was present when they fell. Secondly, these demons recognized the authority of Jesus their creator. This is significant, in that when we feel oppressed, we must remember that we have a personal relationship with the one who has all authority.

> Praise Him, all His angels; Praise Him, all His hosts! Praise Him, sun and moon; Praise Him, all you stars of light! Praise Him, you heavens of heavens, And you waters above the heavens! Let them praise the name of the LORD, For He commanded and they were created.
>
> –Psalm 148:2-5

In this account we see the creation of the heavens, the earth and the seas. But mentioned even before these are the angels of heaven.

ANGELS ARE INVISIBLE

That is, they are invisible according to the human abilities of perception. The above passage from Colossians says "by him (Jesus) all things were created that are in heaven and that are on the earth, visible and *invisible."* There are things that are seen and things that are not. Look at a description of angels from Hebrews Chapter one:

> But to which of the angels has He ever said: "Sit at My right hand, till I make Your enemies Your footstool"? Are they not all ministering **spirits** sent forth to minister for those who will inherit salvation?
>
> -Hebrews 1:14

Again we read:

> He lays the beams of His upper chambers in the waters, Who makes the clouds His chariot, Who walks on the wings of the wind, Who makes His angels **spirits**, His ministers a flame of fire.
>
> –Psalm 104:4

Angels are spirits. They are made of "spirit stuff." And we know from the testimony of Christ, Himself "...a spirit does not have flesh and bones as you see I have" -Luke 24:39. Angels are invisible.

ANGELS ARE HIGHER THAN MAN

They were created before man, and they are a higher creature than we. Psalm 8:4-5 says,

> What is man that You are mindful of him, and the son of man that You visit him? For You have made him a little lower than the angels, and You have crowned him with glory and honor.

God has made the angels higher than man, or to put it as the psalmist did, man has been made a little lower that the angels. In 2 Samuel David, King of Israel received a compliment from the woman of Tokoa, "but my lord *is* wise, according to the wisdom of the angel of God, to know everything that *is* in the earth." –2 Samuel 14:20.

ANGELS ARE POWERFUL

There are two major passages that discuss the power of the angels. Peter wrote,

> ...whereas angels, who are greater in power and might (than man), do not bring a reviling accusation against them before the Lord.
> -2Peter 2:11

We read in Psalm 103:20,

> Bless the LORD, you His angels, who **excel in strength**, who do His word, heeding the voice of His word.

Even though angels are creatures of great power, they remain created creatures, and are not to receive worship. The Apostle Paul wrote:

> Let no one cheat you of your reward, taking delight in false humility and worship of angels, intruding into those things, which he has not seen, vainly puffed up by his fleshly mind,

While on the isle of Patmos, John the apostle received the Revelation of Jesus Christ. He fell down to worship the angel who was so great and mighty and had reveled so much to him:

> And I fell at his feet to worship him. But he said to me, "See that you do not do that! I am your fellow servant, and of your brethren who have

> the testimony of Jesus. Worship God! For the testimony of Jesus is the spirit of prophecy."
>
> -Revelation 19:10

Keeping in mind that we are NOT to worship angels, which are created higher than man, we certainly are not to worship Mary or any other human being.

ANGELS ARE NUMEROUS

Angels are large in number. In fact they are as great in number as the stars in the sky. This is the impression that we get from the Word of God.

> But you have come to Mount Zion and to the city of the living God, the heavenly Jerusalem, to an innumerable company of angels,
>
> -Hebrews 12:22

Innumerable means that you cannot count them. There are more angels than there are numbers. The Apostle John describes his experience in Revelation 5:11.

> Then I looked, and I heard the voice of many angels around the throne, the living creatures, and the elders; and the number of them was ten thousand times ten thousand, and thousands of thousands,

John said that he saw angels around the throne of God, and then he saw angels circled in a ring, then a ring beyond them and beyond them. John finally finishes by saying, And there were myriads and myriads of angels." He could not count them, there were so many.

ANGELS ARE SEXLESS

Unlike the angels that one sees on the front of a hallmark card, angels are not men or women. They are sexless. The angels according to Jesus, neither marry nor are given in marriage (Mark 12:25). As far as is known from Scripture, they do not in any way reproduce but were created with a specific number that remain today. We can assume from Colossians 1:16-17 that their number never increases nor decreases.

WHO ARE ANGELS?

THE WORD ANGEL CAN APPLY TO GOD

It is important to notice all of the uses of the word a*ngelos*. The word actually applies to God in some cases. In the Old Testament we find appearances of the Angel of the LORD or the Angel of Jehovah (YHWH).

> Now the Angel of the LORD found her (Hagar) by a spring of water in the wilderness, by the spring on the way to Shur. And He said, "Hagar, Sarai's maid, where have you come from, and where are you going?" She said, "I am fleeing from the presence of my mistress Sarai." The Angel of the LORD said to her, "Return to your mistress, and submit yourself under her hand." Then the Angel of the LORD said to her, "I will multiply your descendants exceedingly, so that they shall not be counted for multitude." And the Angel of the LORD said to her:
>
> -Genesis 16:7-11

The Angel of the LORD here, is God and many believe that the term Angel of Jehovah in the Old Testament refers to none other than the preincarnate Christ.

THE WORD ANGEL CAN APPLY TO MEN

Men are called angels. This can be found in many Scriptures. On one occasion John the Baptist sent two of his disciples as messengers with a question for Jesus. When they got their answer the messengers returned to John with the answer.

> When the **messengers** of John had departed, He began to speak to the multitudes concerning John: "What did you go out into the wilderness to see? A reed shaken by the wind?
>
> -Luke 7:24

The word here translated as messengers is *angelos*. It could have legitimately been translated *"When the **angels** of John had departed..."*

In James 2:25:

> Likewise, was not Rahab the harlot also justified by works when she received the messengers and sent *them* out another way?

Here the Spies of Israel are called "angels." All of the greetings to the "seven angels" of the seven churches in Revelation 2 & 3 are probably not spirit beings assigned to these churches but the human messengers or pastors. If *angelos* in these passages were to refer to spirit beings, why did Christ use John as the go between? Why did He not just communicate directly to these spirits who minister to Him.

THE WORD ANGEL CAN APPLY TO MEN

There are times that the word *angelos* is used for the departed spirit of a man. This is probably where we came up with the convoluted idea that men become angels when they die. However it is clear from Scripture that this is not the case. In the book of Acts, Luke the physician records such an occasion. Peter was incarcerated and the church was praying for his release. An angel appeared to him and released him from jail just as the church had asked. He arrived at the location of the prayer meeting and a girl told these faithful saints that he was outside.

> But they said to her, "You are beside yourself!" Yet she kept insisting that it was so. So they said, "It is his **angel**."
>
> -Acts 12:15

They said *angelos* but they were referring to his spirit. Another example is found in Matthew 18:10:

> Take heed that you do not despise one of these little ones, for I say to you that in heaven their **angels** always see the face of My Father who is in heaven.

This cannot be used to develop the false view that departed spirits become angels. Look at Hebrews 12:22-23:

> But you have come to Mount Zion and to the city of the living God, the heavenly Jerusalem, to an innumerable company of angels, to the general assembly and church of the firstborn who are registered in heaven, to God the Judge of all, to the spirits of just men made perfect,

These verses make it clear that the angels and spirits of men are brought into the presence of God together and remain separate.

How do Angels Relate?

What is the Angel's Relation to the Earth and to the Human Family?

Angels desire to look into the gospel (1 Peter 1:12). They were present at the giving of the Law (Galatians 3:19). They were present at the birth of Christ—"a multitude of the heavenly host praising God" (Luke2:9-14). Angels have ministered to men and to Christ. The writer of Hebrews says that angels are: "ministering spirits sent forth to minister for those who will inherit salvation" (Hebrews 1:14).

How do angel rank?

Angels are arranged according to orders. The have ranks much like the military. Michael is the archangel. He is the mighty one who stands for the children of Israel. He is mentioned in the book of Daniel and again in Revelation.

Gabriel is not an archangel. Gabriel is apparently an angel who is a special messenger for God. He came to Daniel to explain the vision of the end times, which God had given him. He had the honor of announcing the births of John the Baptist and Jesus Christ.

Then there are the cherubim who honor God's holiness and were placed in the Garden of Eden to guard the entrance. Later, in the tabernacle it was the golden cherubim that guarded the mercy seat of God.

In Isaiah 6:1-8 we are introduced to the seraphim, standing about the throne of God in worship and purpose.

Now turning to Ephesians 1:21, notice that Paul lists "all principality and power and might and dominion." These are grades of angels.

CONCLUSION

Angels are the created spirits who minister to man and God. They are the guardians of those who will inherit eternal life, and they praise God day and night. They are invisible beings that are a little higher than man, yet they long to know the grace of Christ as we know it. All said and done, I am thankful that I am a saint but not an angel.

Dispensationalism

The essence of Dispensationalism is the distinction between Israel and the Church. This grows out of the dispensationalists' consistent employment of normal or plain interpretation, and it reflects an understanding of the basic purpose of God in all His dealings with mankind as that of glorifying Himself through salvation and other purposes as well.

-Charles C. Ryrie, Dispensationalism

Glossary

In order to best conduct a study of the Doctrine of Dispensationalism, it is first imperative to define the terminology that is common to this area of theology. For this reason, the glossary precedes any discussion of the actual teaching of Dispensational Theology.

Age- A period of time or a dispensation. In the above sense the word occurs only once in the King James Version, in the sing, as the translation of, *dor*, which means, properly, a "revolution" or "round of time," "a period," "an age" or "generation of man's life"; almost invariable translated "generation," "generations" (Job 8:8, "Inquire, I pray thee, of the former age"); we have the plural as the translation of aion, properly "duration," "the course or flow of time," "an age or period of the world," "the world" (Eph 2:7, "in the ages to come"; Col 1:26, "the mystery which hath been hid from ages and from generations," the English Revised Version, "from all ages," etc., the American Revised Version, margin, of genea, "generations" (Eph 3:5 "generations," Eph 3:21, "unto all generations for ever and ever," Greek margin, "all the generations of the age of the ages"). "Ages" is given in margin of the King James Version (Ps 145:13; Isa 26:4, "the rock of ages").

–W. L. Walker[37]

Amillinnialism- The teaching that there will be no literal millennium following Christ's return to earth.

Biblical Covenants- "A Biblical covenant is an agreement or contract between God and a specific group of people. There is a distinction between man-made covenants during Biblical eras and Biblical covenants made by the Lord God."[38] There are five covenants that God made with Israel.

---

[37] Orr James, *International Standard Bible Encyclopedia*: Cedar Rapids Parsons Technology, Inc.
[38] Dr. George Hare, *Biblical Hermeneutics*, Supplement #2.

Church- The church consists of the whole number of the elect that have been, are, or shall be gathered into one under Christ, the head thereof. This is a pure society, the church in which Christ dwells. It is the body of Christ. It is called "invisible" because the greater part of those who constitute it are already in heaven or are yet unborn, and also because its members still on earth cannot certainly be distinguished. The qualifications of membership in it are internal and are hidden. It is unseen except by Him who "searches the heart." "The Lord knoweth them that are his" (2 Tim. 2:19). [39] Or as Charles Colson said it: "Biblically the church is an organism not an organization—a movement, not a monument. It is not a part of the community; it is a whole new community. It is not an orderly gathering; it is a new order with new values, often in sharp conflict with the values of the surrounding society."[40]

Covenant Theology- A system of theology teaching that God entered into a covenant of works with Adam, who failed, whereupon God entered into a covenant of grace, promising eternal life to those who believe. Covenant theology affirms there is one people of God called true Israel, the church (in contrast to dispensationalism, which teaches there are two people of God, called Israel and the church).

Dispensation- An administration, ministry, or stewardship for which a person has responsibility in God's administration of salvation. In certain interpretations of Scripture, a period of time during which people are tested in respect to their obedience to a specific revelation of God's will.[41]

Dispensationalism- Dispensationalism is the result of a system of interpretation that seeks to establish a unity in the Scriptures through its central focus on the grace of God. Although dispensationalists recognize differing stewardships or

---

[39] M. G. Easton, *Easton's Bible Dictionary*, s.v. "Church."
[40] Edythe Draper, *Draper's Quotations for the Christian Word:* Wheaton IL. Tyndale House Publisher
[41] *Holman Bible Dictionary*, s.v. "Dispensation."

dispensations whereby the Lord put man under a trust, they teach that response to God's revelation in each dispensation is by faith (salvation is *always* by grace through faith). Dispensationalists arrive at their system of interpretation through two primary principles: (1) maintaining a consistently literal method of interpretation, and (2) maintaining a distinction between Israel and the church.

Hermeneutics- Hermeneutics is the science of interpreting the Bible (or any piece of literature). The word comes from a Greek word, hermeneuo, which means to interpret or to explain.

Postmillennialism- This view holds that the world will become progressively better with the ultimate triumph of the gospel. Christ will return after the millennium. It is presently being revived in "Christian Reconstructionism."[42]

Posttribuilationalism- The belief that the church will be on earth during the Tribulation; it will not be raptured away.[43]

Premillennialism- Premillennialists hold that Jesus will return before ("pre-") He establishes a millennial kingdom on this earth. This return will be necessary because forces hostile to God will be governing the world, and Christ must conquer them before He can rule. Towards the end of the millennium evil will again arise, and it will have to be defeated once more before God's cosmic rule is perfected. Until the fourth century, the early church was generally premillennial. This perspective, which placed the church in sharp conflict with the Roman Empire, declined rapidly after Constantine made Christianity the Empire's favored religion. In subsequent centuries radical groups at odds with state-supported religion often held premillennialism.[44]

---

[42] Paul Enns, *The Moody Handbook of Theology,* Moody Press, Chicago IL.
[43] Ibid.
[44] *Holman Bible Dictionary,* s.v. "Eschatology/The Millennium."

Pretribulationalism- The belief that Christ will rapture the church before the tribulation.[45]

Progressive Dispensationalism- Progressive Dispensationalists pronounce themselves a legitimate development within dispensationalism. However, it appears that they are a distinct difference from classic dispensationalism.

Progressive revelation- God did not reveal all truth about Himself at one time but revealed Himself "piecemeal," portion by portion to different people throughout history (cf. Heb. 1:1).[46]

Steward- In a dispensation one of the requirements is a person to whom God imparts the responsibility to manage the details of that particular economy.

Stewardship- Utilizing and managing all resources God provides for the glory of God and the betterment of His creation.

Ultradispensationalism- Classic Dispensationalism places the beginning of the Church age at the day of Pentecost as seen in Acts chapter 2. There are two opposing views within Dispensationalism called Ultradispensationalism. First is the view that the Church age began in Acts 13 with the Apostle Paul's first missionary journey. The second holds to the view that it did not begin until Acts 28, at the end of Paul's mission.

---

[45] Paul Enns, *The Moody Handbook of Theology*, Moody Press, Chicago IL. 643.
[46] Ibid

Dispensationalism Introduced

Dispensational theology is not without its opponents. Though the natural result of a literal grammatical historical hermeneutic, many refuse to acknowledge its truths. One opponent put it this way:

> "Dispensationalism refers to the extrabiblical view that God changes His ways and His mind in different eras of history. It feeds the erroneous view of *modalism*, which is an evolutionary view of God, and is ultimately defeatist in outlook. Dispensationalism ignores or denies the unity of the New-Testament church with the people of God from history past, namely the descendants of Abraham; and seems to wink at all the evidence that God is immutable: never-changing. It is important to note that dispensationalism is a distinctly twentieth-century phenomenon, thanks to such influences as Scofield's Bible notes -- as well as the naturally escapist tendencies we share as fallen men."
>
> -James Pavlic

Sadly this type of unwarranted and unknowledgeable attack is not uncommon it theological circles. When coming up against such attacks the unashamed Christian must have valid answers.

First we must understand a crucial truth. Dispensationalism is not a method of interpretation as its opponents would have us believe, but it is merely the result of a literal grammatical historical hermeneutic.

There are six primary ideas that we will be considering to assist us in our study of dispensational theology; these are not the only areas of impact in this theology but the primary focus of this study.

1. Hermeneutically, dispensationalism follows an *unswervingly* literal, grammatical historical approach to interpretation of the Scripture. Other systems like covenant theology admit to basic hermeneutical changes within their interpretations of the Bible based on now definitive rules of interpretation. This leads to an allegorical interpretation, which can lead to dangerous conclusions and miss-applications.

2. Dispensationalism has an ability to recognize the changing economies or dispensations throughout biblical history. This feature has led to maintaining a clear distinction between God's programs for Israel and for the church.

3. Dispensationalism is based on legitimate biblical ideas of differing economies (Ephesians 1:10; 3:2, 9; etc.). It can be shown that there are seven possible different dispensations.

4. True dispensationalism cannot be mistaken for ultradispensationalism. This extreme outside group in its most radical form has restricted applicable Scriptures to some of Paul's epistles. They reject both baptism and the Lord's Supper. The main problem with this model is its failure to recognize the beginning of the church at Pentecost (Acts 2). They instead place the beginning of the church depending on which ultradispensational faction is consulted, in Acts 9, 13, or 28.

5. Dispensationalism focuses on the glory of God instead of the salvation of man as the objective of all things. It centers on God, not man. Regardless of what the established educational establishment would have us

believe, man is NOT the center of all. God's primary purpose in this world is the glory of God.

6. A misunderstanding concerning the way of salvation has sometimes been applied to dispensationalism. Some opponents have wrongly thought that dispensationalism teaches that the way of salvation has differed from one dispensation to another. It is true that the object which men placed their faith in has changed from dispensation to dispensation, yet in every age salvation has been by God's grace through man's faith.

In identifying a dispensation there are eight separate yet connected components that one must recognize. First one needs to be able to identify the *steward* or key person whom God has delegated the responsibility of the administration of the dispensation. Secondly, there must be an identifiable *period*, with a beginning and an end. Third, one must be able to determine the group of *people* that are governed within the dispensation. For instance does the dispensation deal with Israel alone, the Church or all of mankind. Next is the *responsibility,* what was the righteous requirement that was placed on the people under that particular dispensation. What was the required act or prohibition? Then one seeks to discover God's method of *testing* His people. As is predictable there soon follows man's *failure.* Not one dispensation has passed that has not resulted in man's failure. After failure comes the righteous *judgment* of God. God is holy and as such He must judge wickedness. The final component that we discover is the evidence of God's *grace.*

Employing a literal interpretation of the Scriptures, resulting in the discovery of the above components produces seven distinct economies or dispensations throughout the Biblical record.

1. Beginning with the creation of Adam and ending with his temptation and fall we find the dispensation of *innocence*. Adam administered this dispensation and the people under its influence were Adam and Eve. Man was in his ideal state; he was innocent (Gen 2:17,25; 3:5). His home was in the beautiful garden at Eden (Gen 2:8), and all of his needs freely supplied (Gen 1:29; 2:9,16). He enjoyed personal fellowship with God (Gen 3:8) and foreknew the consequences of his disobedience (Gen 2:17). The responsibility was simple. Exercise authority over creation, be fruitful and multiply and do not eat of the tree of knowledge of good and evil. Would man obey these instructions and honor the daily personal revelation received from the Lord Himself? We all know the answer; it comes in Adam's crushing failure (Gen 3:1-6). Satan himself tempted man to sin against God using the lust of the flesh, the lust of the eyes and the pride of life (Gen 3:5). This was his method with the first humans and it has not changed. Judgment follows failure. In Romans 5:12 and 6:23 Paul the Apostle explains the judgment that followed Adams failure.

> Therefore, just as through one man sin entered the world, and death through sin, and thus death spread to all men, because all sinned— For the wages of sin *is* death, but the gift of God *is* eternal life in Christ Jesus our Lord.

Due to the sin of Adam death entered the world "the wages of sin is death" and that death spread to all mankind. However, just as judgment follows failure, God is never short on grace. Had it not been for the grace of God the entire human race (both of them) would have been wiped out. It is also notable that it was at this time of judgment that God promised a savior (Gen 3:15).

2. God's next economy began with Adam's fall and expulsion and continued until the flood. The dispensation of *conscience* was a time when God dealt with the entire human race. The stewards were probably the heads of the family units of Adam's descendants. There is evidence in Scripture that would indicate that God dealt with men through the head of the family. We see this type of rule indicated in Job. This was prominent until the period of the law, though God still dealt largely with the family. These men guided by conscience were to choose to do good and to approach God by means of sacrifice, as given in the divine example in the garden, (Gen 3:21; 4:4,7). So comes the question, would man fear God and avoid evil on the basis of Conscience? The failure was described in Genesis 6:5:

> Then the LORD saw that the wickedness of man *was* great in the earth, and *that* every intent of the thoughts of his heart *was* only evil continually.

As is the case with sin, God judged evil mankind and brought on the flood. In the wake of this disaster it might be difficult to see God's grace, however it is evident. Noah and his family were spared despite the sins of mankind.

3. Dr. George Hare describes the beginning of the dispensation of *human government* as follows:

> The beginning of this dispensation finds just eight people living, all of whom know God. Undoubtedly great changes in the earth were present at this time. Apparently the water ice canopy encircling the earth had collapsed, providing flood rains. Now for the first time man is faced with sun rays which aided in shortening his life span. For the first time

seasons occur (Gen 8:21-22). Noah and his family began the race a second time[47].

Noah was the steward of this dispensation. God dealt directly with him, giving him instructions for the world (Genesis 8:20; 9:17). This period began with the flood and ended with the confusion of tongues at the Tower of Babel. God had for the first time instituted human government with the responsibility of upholding God's righteous requirements up to and including the taking of human life. The question was posed, would man by means of government keep himself well-pleasing before God, cause righteousness to rule in the earth, and scattering abroad populate the earth? The answer is of course, no. This dispensation closes with sin again rampant and the race under God's disapproval. He responded by dividing them into different languages, dividing the earth into separated continents. God yet demonstrated His grace to these through his willingness to spare mankind again.

4. Abraham ushered in the following dispensation, the dispensation of *promise*. As the steward, Abraham alone had the responsibility to father a promised nation. The promise of a nation was passed from father to son through Jacob whose name was changed to Israel. Beginning with the call of Abraham it extended to the failure at Mount Sinai. This particular dispensation passed by the whole of humanity for a select group of people, namely Abraham and his descendants. This is the point where God began dealing with His chosen people who were destined to become His nation (Exodus 19:4-6). Those who were under this dispensation were to believe and serve God whether they prospectively, partially or entirely possessed the great spiritual, material and social promises given to Abraham. Again, as always comes the test. Would the nation of Israel, even in adverse circumstances, believe the

---

[47] Hare, George, *Dispensationalism Class Notes*: El Cajon Ca. SCBC&S

promises God gave to Abraham that they would be a great nation under God's particular guidance and protection? Well, it comes as no surprise that in each phase the men failed. God, as always judged the sins of those under this dispensation. God separated Himself from them in contrast to His previous nearness to them. And as always, God's grace is evident in His provision for Israel through Moses and the Passover.

5. By far the most stringent dispensation began at the giving of the *Law* and continued until the death of the Messiah. There were several stewards during this time, beginning with Moses and continuing through the prophets. Again, this dispensation was for the nation Israel and a few select proselyte gentiles. God made it clear; Israel was to live under the rule of law by meeting the requirements set out in it. This was so that the rest of the nations would see that they were God's people (Deuteronomy 4:1-8, 28:10). Israel was a complete failure; they were not able to live under the rule of law as a testimony to the other nations. Judgment came in a series of conquests beginning with Assyria and never really ending. God demonstrated His righteous grace through a variety of means. Judges were raised up to rescue them, kings to lead them in battle and prophets to warn them against sin and impending judgment.

6. Paul the Apostle was the principal agent of the revelation of the *Grace* of God for this dispensation. Jesus Himself brought the grace of God to mankind in His incarnation (Titus 2:11), but Paul was the person who taught it. This is not to say that there was no grace in the previous dispensations. In fact, we have already shown that God allowed His grace to shine throughout the ages. Man has a responsibility under grace; accept the gift (Romans 5:15-18). God has now begun to deal with the entire human race again, no longer just with Israel. There is in this current dispensation still a failure, the vast majority of those living

in this era will reject Christ and as a result they will be judged. When Christ returns that will draw to a close this present time of grace and those Christ rejecters who are still living, will be judged.

7. The final dispensation will come at Christ's triumphant return and the setting up of the *millennial kingdom*. It will end with the final rebellion of Gog and Magog. Jesus Himself will rule and reign as steward of this final period in human history. All mankind will be under His rule and He will demand total obedience. Having provided the perfect living environment, man will be responsible to simply be obedient from the heart and to remain undefiled. And of course there will be a failure. We read about it in Revelation 20:7-9.

> Now when the thousand years have expired, Satan will be released from his prison and will go out to deceive the nations which are in the four corners of the earth, Gog and Magog, to gather them together to battle, whose number *is* as the sand of the sea. They went up on the breadth of the earth and surrounded the camp of the saints and the beloved city. And fire came down from God out of heaven and devoured them.

The climax of the kingdom is the defeat of the rebellion and of Satan, when he is cast into the lake of fire with all of his demons forever. Those sinful men that refuse to bow to the righteousness of Christ will too be cast into everlasting torment. God's righteousness is even present here with the righteous rule of Christ for one thousand years as well as the perfect living environment that will exist in the absence of Satan.

Conclusion

Dispensationalism is a theological truth that causes much heated debate. Both sides claim to have a handle on the truth, each arriving at it through a different hermeneutic. The final test is a sharp turn to Scripture. Does the Word of God support differing methods of rule for different persons at different times. That is answered in the positive. With this being the case there are really only two explanations. First, one must conclude that God is some kind hearted; old absent-minded, grandfatherly figure that is not really sure of what he intends to do. Or He is the all sovereign, all knowing, all-powerful creator of the universe and He has a detailed specific plan for all of mankind. I choose the latter.

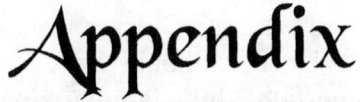

Appendix

God's Lesser Glory:
The Diminished God of "Open Theism"

Journal of the Evangelical Theological Society; Lynchburg; Dec 2001; A Boyd Luter; Emily Hunter;

God's Lesser Glory: The Diminished God of Open Theism. By Bruce A. Ware. Wheaton: Crossway, 2000, 240 pp.

Bruce Ware is Senior Associate Dean of the School of Theology and Professor of Christian Theology at Southern Seminary, Louisville, Kentucky. Perhaps best known as co-editor (with Tom Schreiner) of The Grace of God, The Bondage of the Will (Baker, 1995) and Still Sovereign:

Contemporary Perspectives on Election, Foreknowledge and Grace (Baker, 2000), Ware, however, is anything but a "static" Calvinist. His 1984 Ph.D. dissertation at Fuller was "An Evangelical Reexamination of the Doctrine of the Immutability of God," which research led to "An Evangelical Reformulation of the Doctrine of the Immutability of God" (JETS 29 [1986] 431-46). Thus, Ware has himself proposed creative adjustments to the "classical" theological formulation.

This is an exceedingly important volume. To our knowledge, the only previous book length critique of the openness of God/freewill theism perspective is McGregor Wright's No Room for Sovereignty: What's Wrong with Freewill Theism (IVP, 1996). This appeared prior to John Sanders's The God Who Risks: A Theology of Providence (IVP, 1998) and Greg Boyd's God of the Possible: A Biblical Introduction to the Open View of God (Baker, 2000), both of which have impacted the escalating debate.

God's Lesser Glory consists of three parts. The introduction, "Why You Should Be Concerned," addresses the "so what?" question by familiarizing readers with the mounting controversy surrounding open theism and the theological "hot spots" the book examines. Part one, "What Does Open Theism Propose?" builds directly on the introduction. Ware succinctly deals with the development of open theism as a theological framework and as a departure from the classical Arminian position (chap. 2), then addresses "The Perceived Benefits of Open Theism" (chap. 3).

Part Two, "What's Wrong with Open Theism's View of God?" responds to Boyd's God of the Possible and Sanders's The God Who Risks. In Chapter 4, "Assessing Open Theism's Denial of Exhaustive Divine Foreknowledge," Ware critiques both the exegetical procedure of open theism and its subsequent application to key Scriptural passages often touted by open theists as support for their position. Chapter 5 outlines a "Scriptural Affirmation of Exhaustive Divine Foreknowledge" as Ware presents careful discussions of select passages of Scripture, against which open theists are at pains to argue effectively. Chapter 6 then addresses a minimally noticed difficulty in open theism: "The God Who Risks and the Assault on God's Wisdom."

Part Three exposes the problematic practical ramifications of open theism. Ware discusses how this position harms the Christian's prayer life (chap. 7), results in diminished confidence in God's guidance (chap. 8), and creates outright despair in the midst of suffering and pain (chap. 9). Finally, in his conclusion "God's Greater Glory and Our Everlasting Good," Ware restates the weaknesses of open theism and reasserts the orthodox view of God's sovereignty.

As to its strengths: (1) The irenic and even-handed, yet concerned, tone of Ware's treatment strikes a commendable balance. (2) The sketch in the introductory chapter of how this controversy has developed provides a historical context needed by many readers. (3) Ware's exegesis has a broader range than that of Sanders and Boyd (e.g. careful discussions of such relevant aspects as Genesis 18, Joseph, Job, Isaiah 41-48, Daniel and prophecy in general), exposing their inconsistencies in (so-called "straightforward") hermeneutics/exegesis and, in the process, securing exhaustive foreknowledge. This breadth fits in with the figures Ware cites in footnote 2 on p. 100, which seems to assert that passages favoring the classical view of God's foreknowledge outnumber the "apparent counter-evidence" passages 4,695 to 105. (4) Ware's exegesis also probes deeper than his openness counterparts (e.g. Genesis 3 and 22, plus 2 Kings 20), exposing the shallowness of their thinking by playing out its doctrinal and practical implications. (5) The dramatic openness overbalance to divine immanence is articulated clearly. (6) The thorny problems openness theism creates for Christian living are effectively laid bare.

Though God's Lesser Glory contains no glaring "weaknesses," there are several areas we believe are underdeveloped or overlooked: (1) The exegesis and theological reflection still need to be broader and deeper. For example, Ware does not touch on Eph 1:4 or Rev 13:8, key passages for both Sanders and Boyd. In addition, Saul's rejection in God's plan (1 Samuel 15) could be handled in a more conclusive fashion by referring to Gen 49:10 and the family tree that crowns Ruth. (2) Though it is helpful for Ware to mention his nuanced relational understanding of divine immutability (see his 1986 JETS article), it deserves more in-depth explication, given that the relational angle is a cultural contact point openness is exploiting. (3) Speaking of culture, it is surprising that Ware does not critique the openness viewpoint against its postmodernist backdrop. Since openness writers are quick to accuse classical theists of drinking at the well of Greek philosophy, it is entirely fair to point out the polluted postmodernist air openness thinkers are breathing. (4) Amazingly, there is no mention of "sin" in the entire volume (note the "loud silence" in the index, p. 236). This is undoubtedly due to the fact that openness exponents seldom mention sin and Ware is answering their stated views. However, given that Ware reflects sensitivity to the elevation of man that is openness's other-side-of-the-coin to the humanizing of God, this is a notable "big picture" absence for a theologian of Ware's acumen.

In conclusion, given what is at stake, God's Lesser Glory has not received the visibility it deserves. As the readership of openness theism books (supporters, detractors and the ranks of the curious) grows with each successive volume, there must be solid answers readily available to the wide-ranging assertions and radical implications of this thought. Until other up-to-date and focused book-length critiques that are in process appear, Ware's treatment admirably meets those educational and apologetic needs.

Though not quite as readable as Boyd's God of the Possible, Ware's writing style is still accessible to readers ranging from scholars to pastors to seminary and Bible college students to high lay level (especially Sunday school and Bible study teachers). As the storm clouds of the first great evangelical theological controversy of the twenty-first century gather, God's Lesser Glory should be considered "required reading" in all these categories, on both sides of the dispute.

[Author note]
A. Boyd Luter and Emily Hunter The Criswell College, Dallas, TX

Selected Bibliography

Aland, Kurt. *The Greek New Testament with Dictionary.* Edmonds: United Bible Society 1966

Anders, Max. *30 Days to Understanding the Bible.* Dallas: Word 1988

_____. *30 Days to Understanding the Christian Life in 15 Minutes a Day!* Nashville: Nelson 1990

_____. *30 Days to Understanding What Christians Believe.* Nashville: Thomas Nelson 1994

_____. *New Christian's Handbook.* Nashville: Nelson 1999

Anderson, Ken. *Where to Find it in the Bible.* Nashville: Nelson 1996

Austin, Steven A. - Ed. *Grand Canyon.* Santee: ICR 1994

Barnes, Peter. *Out of Darkness into Light.* San Diego: Equippers 1984

_____. *The Truth about Jesus and the Trinity.* San Diego: Equipper's 1989

Blomberg, Craig. *1 Corinthians.* Grand Rapids: Zondervan 1995

Booth, A. E. *The Course of Time from Eternity to Eternity.* Neptune: Loizeaux Brothers

Braga, James. *How to Study the Bible.* Portland: Multnomah 1982

Brown, Francis and et al. *The Brown-Driver-Briggs Hebrew and English Lexicon.* Peabody: Hendrickson 1999

Bruce, A. B. *The Training of the Twelve.* Grand Rapids: Kregel 1971

Bryant, T. Alton - Ed. *Compact Bible Dictionary.* Grand Rapids: Regency 1967

Bullinger, E. W. *Figures of Speech Used in the Bible.* Grand Rapids: Baker 1968

Bullock, C. Hassell. *An Introduction to the Old Testament Prophetic Books.* Chicago: Moody 1986

Burton, Sam Westman. *Disciple Mentoring.* Pasadena: William Carey 2000

Cairns, Earle E. *Christianity through the Centuries.* Grand Rapids: Zondervan 1954

Chafer, Lewis Sperry. *Grace.* Grand Rapids: Kregel 1922

———. *He that is Spiritual.* Grand Rapids: Zondervan 1918

———. *Salvation.* Grand Rapids: Kregel 1991

———. *Satan.* Grand Rapids: Kregel 1990

———. *Systematic Theology 1- 8 set.* Kregel

Cole, R. Alan. *Galatians.* Grand Rapids: IVP / Eerdmans 1965

Comfort, Philip Wesley - Ed. *The Origin of the Bible.* Wheaton: Tyndale

Cooper, Lamar Eugene. *The New American Commentary (Ezekiel).* Broadman & Holman 1994

Corduan, Winfried. *Neighboring Faiths.* Downers Grove: IVP 1998

Couch, Mal. *The Fundamentals for the Twenty-First Century.* Grand Rapids: Kregel 2000

Cox, Steven. *Essentials of New Testament Greek - A Student's Guide.* Broadman & Holman

Dana, H. E. and Julius R. Mantey. *A Manual Grammar of the Greek New Testament.* Upper Saddle River: Prentice Hall 1927

Davidson, Benjamin. *The Analytical Hebrew and Chaldee Lexicon.* Zondervan

Dickason, C. Fred. *Demon Possession & the Christian.* Crossway

Dueck, Alvin C. *Between Jerusalem & Athens.* Grand Rapids: Baker 1995

Edersheim, Alfred. *Bible History - Old Testament.* Peabody: Hendrickson 1995

_____. *The Life and Times of Jesus the Messiah.* Detroit: Hendrickson Publishers 1993.

Eibfeldt, O. *Liber Genesis.* Vierte: Deutsche Biblegesellschaft – Stuttgart 1969

Elliger, K. *Biblia Hebraica – Stuttgartensia.* Deutsche Biblegesellschaft 1969

Elwell, Walter A. *Evangelical Dictionary of Theology.* Cumbria: Baker 1984

Enns, Paul. *The Moody Handbook of Theology.* Chicago: Moody 1989

Evans, Tony. *America's Only Hope.* Chicago: Moody 1990

_____. *Are Christians Destroying America?* Chicago: Moody 1996

_____. *Our God is Awesome.* Chicago: Moody 1994

Foulkes, Francis. *Ephesians.* Grand Rapids: IVP / Eerdmans 1963

Geisler, Norman L. *A General Introduction to the Bible.* Chicago: Moody 1968

_____. and William E. Nix. *From God to Us.* Chicago: Moody 1974

_____. *Christian Apologetics.* Grand Rapids: Baker

Gish, Duane T. *Evolution: the Fossils Still Say No!* El Cajon: ICR 1995

Gonzalez, Justo. *The Story of Christianity - Volume 2.* New York: Harpercollins 1985

Grassmick, John D. *Principles and Practice of Greek Exegesis* Dallas: Dallas Theological Seminary 1974

Greenberg, Moshe. *Introduction to Hebrew.* Englewood Cliffs: Prentice Hall 1965

Grunlan, Stephen A. & Marvin K. Mayers. *Cultural Anthropology.* Grand Rapids: Zondervan 1979

Halley, Henry H. *Halley's Bible Handbook.* Grand Rapids: Zondervan 1927

Hastings, James - Ed. *Hastings' Dictionary of the Bible.* New York: Hendrickson 1909

Hester, H. I. *The Heart of Hebrew History.* Nashville: Broadman 1962

Hodges, C. Zane. *The Greek New Testament according to the Majority Text.* Nashville: Nelson 1985

Hoekema, Anthony A. *Created in God's Image.* Grand Rapids: Eerdmans 1986

_____. *Saved by Grace.* Grand Rapids: Eerdmans 1989

_____. *The Bible and the Future.* Grand Rapids: Eerdmans 1979

Hoerth, Alfred J. *Archaeology & the Old Testament.* Grand Rapids: Baker 1998

House, H. Wayne - Ed. *Chronological and Background Charts of the New Testament.* Grand Rapids: Zondervan 1981

_____. and Kenneth M. Durharn. *Living Wisely in a Foolish World.* Grand Rapids: Kregel 1992

Hughes, R. Kent. *Disciplines of a Godly Man.* Wheaton: Crossway 1991

Hutchcraft, Ron. *The Battle for a Generation.* Chicago: Moody 1996

Ice, Thomas and Timothy Demy. *Fast Facts on Bible Prophecy.* Eugene: Harvest 1997

Jensen, Irving L. *Jensen's Survey of the New Testament.* Chicago: Moody 1981

_____. *Jensen's Survey of the Old Testament.* Chicago: Moody 1978

Jeremiah, David. *Core Values of the Church.* San Diego: Turning point 1996

_____. *The Handwriting on the Wall.* Dallas: Word 1992

Kelley, Page H. *Biblical Hebrew.* Grand Rapids: Eerdmans 1992

Kent, Homer A. *A Heart Opened Wide - Studies in 2 Corinthians.* Winona Lake: BMH Books 1982

_____. *Faith that Works.* Winona Lake: BMH Books 1986

_____. *Jerusalem to Rome Studies in Acts.* Grand Rapids: Baker 1972

_____. *Light in the Darkness.* Winona Lake: BMH Books 1974

_____. *The Epistle to the Hebrews.* Winona Lake: BMH Books 1972

_____. *The Freedom of God's Sons.* Winona Lake: BMH Books 1976

_____. *The Pastoral Epistles (1 & 2 Timothy and Titus).* *Winona Lake:* BMH Books 1986

_____. *Treasures of Wisdom.* Winona Lake: BMH Books 1978

Kubo, Sakae. *A Reader's Greek-English Lexicon of the New Testament.* Zondervan

Larkin, Clarence. *The Book of Revelation.* REV. Clarence Larkin Estate

Lightfoot, J. B. *Biblical Essays.* Hendrickson 1893

Little, Paul. *How to Give Away Your Faith.* Downers Grove: IVP 1966

Lubenow, Marvin L. *Bones of Contention.* Grand Rapids: Baker 1992

MacArthur, John F. and Wayne A. Mack. *Ashamed of the Gospel.* Wheaton: Crossway 1993

_____. *The Master's Plan for the Church.* Moody

_____. *Our Sufficiency in Christ.* Dallas: Word Publishing 1991.

McCallum, Dennis - Ed. *The Death of Truth.* Minneapolis: Bethany House 1996

McClain, Alva J. *Romans.* Winona Lake: BMH Books 1973

_____. *The Greatness of the Kingdom.* BMH Books

McDonald, Lee M. *The Formation of the Christian Biblical Canon.* Peabody: 1995

McDowell, Josh. *A Ready Defense.* Nashville: Nelson 1993

McGee, J. Vernon *Evidence that Demands a Verdict.* Nashville: Nelson 1975

_____.. *The Best of J. Vernon McGee. Volume 1.* Nashville: Thomas

Nelson 1988.

_____. *Doctrine for Difficult Days.* Nashville: Thomas Nelson

publishers 1996

_____. *Jesus: Centerpiece of Scripture.* Nashville: Thomas Nelson

publishers 1995.

_____. *On Prophecy: Man's Fascination with the Future.* Nashville:

Thomas Nelson Publishers 1993

_____. *Thru the Bible with J. Vernon McGee.* Nashville: Thomas Nelson Publishers 1981.

_____. *Jesus: Centerpiece of Scripture.* Nashville: Thomas Nelson publishers 1995.

Morris, Henry M. *Creation and the Modern Christian.* El Cajon: Master Book 1985

_____. *Many Evidences for the Infallible Christian Faith Proofs.* Green Forest: Master Books 1974

_____. *Science and the Bible.* Chicago: Moody 1951

_____. *Scientific Creationism.* El Cajon: Master books 1974

_____. *The Biblical Basis for Modern Science.* Grand Rapids: Baker 1984

_____. *The Genesis Record.* Grand Rapids: Baker 1976

_____. *The Long War against God.* Grand Rapids: Baker 1989

_____. *What is Creation Science?* El Cajon: Master books 1982

Morris, Leon. *1 & 2 Thessalonians.* Grand Rapids: IVP / Eerdmans 1956

Pentecost, J. Dwight. *Things to Come.* Grand Rapids: Zondervan 1958

Perschbacher, Wesley J. *The New Analytical Greek Lexicon.* Peabody: Hendrickson 1990

Radmacher, Earl and et al - Eds. *New Illustrated Bible Commentary.* Nashville: Nelson 1999

Ramm, Bernard. *Protestant Biblical Interpretation.* Grand Rapids: Baker 1970

Reed, David A. *Answering Jehovah's Witnesses.* Grand Rapids: Baker 1996

Robertson, Archibald. *Word Pictures in the New Testament Set 1 – 6.* Broadman

Rogers, Perry M. *Aspects of Western Civilization.* Englewood Cliffs: Prentice Hall 1988

Ryken, Leland. *How to Read the Bible as Literature.* Grand Rapids: Academic Books 1984

Ryrie, Charles C. *Balancing the Christian Life.* Chicago: Moody 1969

_____. *Basic Theology.* Chicago: Moody 1986

_____. *Dispensationalism.* Chicago: Moody 1966

_____. *Ryrie Study Bible Expanded Edition KJV.* Moody

_____. *Ryrie Study Bible Expanded Edition NAS.* Moody

_____. *So Great Salvation.* Chicago: Moody 1997

_____. *The Basis of the Premillinnial Faith.* Neptune: Loizeaux Brothers 1953

_____. *The Holy Spirit.* Chicago: Moody 1965

Saucy, Robert L. *The Church in God's Program.* Chicago: Moody 1972

Strong, James. *The New Strong's Exhaustive Concordance of the Bible.* Nashville: Nelson 1964

Spurgeon, C.H. *The Life and Work of Our Lord* Vol 1-3. Grand Rapids: Baker Books 1904

Summers, Ray. *Essentials of New Testament Greek.* Nashville: Broadman & Holman 1995

Tenney, Merrill C. *Galatians.* Grand Rapids: Eerdmans 1950

Unger, Merrill F. *The New Unger's Bible Dictionary.* Moody

Vine, W. E. *Vine's Complete Expository Dictionary.* Nashville: Nelson 1984

Virkler, Henry. *Hermeneutics.* Grand Rapids: Baker 1981

Wallace, Daniel B. *Greek Grammar Beyond the Basics.* Grand Rapids: Zondervan 1996

Wallace, Daniel B. *The Basics of New Testament Syntax.* Grand Rapids: Zondervan 2000

Walvoord, John F. and Roy B. Zuck. *The Bible Knowledge Commentary (New Testament).* Colorado Springs: Victor 1983

_____. *Daniel - the Key to Prophetic Revelation.* Chicago: Moody 1971

_____. *Jesus Christ Our Lord.* Chicago: Moody 1969

_____. *The Holy Spirit.* Grand Rapids: Zondervan 1954

_____. *The Revelation of Jesus Christ.* Chicago: Moody 1966

_____. *Thy Kingdom Come.* Grand Rapids: Kregel 1974

Whiston, William. *The Works of Josephus.* Peabody: Hendrickson 1987

Whitcomb, John C. *The Early Earth.* Grand Rapids: Baker 1972

_____. *The Genesis Flood.* Grand Rapids: Baker 1961

_____. *The World that Perished.* Grand Rapids: Baker 1988

Wiersbe, Warren W. *The Bible Exposition Commentary.*
   Colorado Springs: Victor 1989

_____. *Wiersbe's Expository Outlines on the New
   Testament.* Colorado Springs:

_____. *Wiersbe's Expository Outlines on the Old
   Testament.* Colorado Springs: Victor 1993

Wigram, George V. and Ralph D. Winter. *The Word Study New
   Testament and Concordance.* Wheaton: Wheaton 1972

Wilberforce, William. *A Practical View of Christianity.*
   Peabody: Hendrickson 1996

Wilkinson, Bruce and Kenneth Boa. *Talk thru the Bible.*
   Nashville: Nelson 1983

_____. *Talk thru Bible Personalities.* Nashville: Walk Thru
   the Bible 1983

Wood, Leon J. *A Survey of Israel's History.* Grand Rapids:
   Zondervan 1970

_____. *The Prophets of Israel.* Grand Rapids: Baker

Woodmorappe, John. *Noah's Ark: a Feasibility Study.* El
   Cajon: ICR 1996

Youngblood, Ronald F., General Editor; F.F. Bruce and R.K.
   Harrison, Consulting

   Editors. *Nelson's New Illustrated Bible Dictionary.*
   Nashville, TN: Thomas

Nelson 1995.

Zodhiates, Spiros. *The Complete Word Study Dictionary of the
   New Testament.* Chattanooga: AMG Publishers 1992

Zuck, Roy B. - Ed. *A Biblical Theology of the New Testament.* Chicago: Moody 1994

_____. - Ed. *A Biblical Theology of the Old Testament.* Chicago: Moody 1991

_____. *Basic Bible Interpretation.* Colorado Springs: Victor 1991

_____. *The Bible Knowledge Commentary 2 Vol. Set.* Colorado Springs: Victor 1983

Subject Index

A

Abraham	12,13,21,43,47,48,59,71,90,108,162,167,168
Abram	89
Adam	108,127,128,154,165,166
Age	28,33,81,87,89,99,108,123,126,128,131,158,161,164,168
Allegorical	163
Alpha	39
Almighty	39,58,120
American Revised Version	158
Amillinnialism	115,158
Ananias	51,57
Angel	23-25,50,86,92,120,122,143-156
Angel of the Lord	92,151
Angelology	143
Angelos	145,151-153

Animation 78,79,100,111
Anthropology 133
Antediluvians 140
Antichrist 117,119,124
Antioch 51,55
Apocrypha 103
Archangel 115,154
Assurance 66-67,70
Assyria 168
Astrology 113
Atheist 134,142
Attributes 27,34,37,41-43,53,83
Authority 16,31,37,54-55,58,79,97-99,102,105
111,146,165
Autographs 97-80,94,96-97,110-111

B

Babylon 92
Balaam 89
Baptism 58-59,163
Barnabas 51,55-56
Beast 45,120,122,124,127
Belshazzar 91-92
Bethlehem 14
Biblical Covenants 158
Biblical Creationism 139,142
Bibliology 55,77-79
Biological Evolution 134,142
Body of Christ 58-59,92,99,159
Book of Life 123-124
Born Again 109,130-131
Boston Herald 128

C

Caesarea 104
Canon 79,101-103,111
Canopy 140,166

Carnal 60,62,82,106
Cell 136-137
Cephas 70
Cherubim 154
Chicago 93
Christ 9-11,22-25,29,36-38,41,44,46,48,50,52
57-62,66-76,78,84-85,87,92,94,97-99,102-104,106,110,114-
115,117-119,121-124,126,129-130,135,143,145,147-148,151-
152,154-155,158,162,165,169
Christian Reconstructionism 160
Christian Science 126
Christology 11
Christophanies 92
Church 51,55-56,62,71,78,82,108,119,121,152-153
157,159-164
Classic Dispensationalism 161
Commandments 29,35,74,85-86,91
Condemnation 31,68,129
Conscience 128-129,166
Cornelius 88
Counsel 39,41-43,140
Covenant 106,117-119,123,158-159,163
Covenant of Grace 159
Covenant Theology 159,163
Creation 32,83-84,93,134,138-142,144-146,161
165,178
Creator 38,98,135,141,145-146,170
Cyprus 56
Cyrene 51,55

D

Daniel 71,89,91,103,118-119,135,154
David 12-15,19,60,71,90,107,123,130,147
Death 12,17-21,31,47,58-59,71-72,104,116-118
124,127-128,165,168
Demon 21,31,33,47,55-57,66,75,84,86,138,145-146
167-169

Devil 22,49,56,69,86,124
Dispensationalism 157-159,161-164,170
Dispensation 99,108,158-161,163-169
Dionysius 69
Disciples 23,36-37,49,54,60,104-105,119,125,151
Dominion 140,145,154
Donkey 17
Dual Authorship 79,95,97

E

Earth 13,32,52,65,76,84,109,116,119-124,134,136
138-141,145-146,148,154,158-160,166-167,169
Egypt 20,30,46,74
Echad 29
Economy 161,163-164,166
Emmaus 104
Emotion 35,54,56-57,100
Empiricism 81-83
English Revised Version 158
Ephesus 65,62
Eschatology 113-114
Essence 27-30,32-34,37,41-43,126,157
Eternal 20-21,24,30,37,41-42,45,47-48,67-68,83
121,124,155,159,165
Evangelical 66,92,96,102,126
Eve 12
Everlasting 14,22,31,46,49,118,169
Evolution 133-139,141-142,158,162
Ezekiel 89

F

Fall 22,24,49-50,74-75,77,127-128,130,165-166
False Prophet 120,124
Father 13,16,18-19,21-22,24,29-31,36-37,43-50
60,84,104-105,116,132,153
Filling 58,62
Firmament 140

Flesh 15,28,37,60,63,68,104,120,129,131,147-148,165
Flood.. 118,166-167
Fossil 137,139
Free 16,41-42,59,68,72,75,78,80,93,95,97,120,130,135

G

Gabriel 154
Galilee 145
Garden of Eden 127,154
Garrett Biblical Institute 88
Gentile 52,122,129,168
Gifts 10,19,41,43,58-59,61-62,68,105,132,165,168
Godhead 83-84
Gog 169
Gospel 28,33,61,66-71,75,84-85,104,129,145,154,160
Goodness 34,84,126
Grace 38,56,58,65-68,71,75,93,155
159-160,164,169
Grammatical 79-80,106-108,162-163
Graphe 96
Great Tribulation 120-121
Great White Throne 123
Grieve 56-57
Guarantee 61,98
Guilt 128-130

H

Hades 117,124
Hagar 151
Hamartiology 125
Heart Language 110-111
Heaven 19,23,28,32,34,50,65-66,83-84,104,109,115-116
119-124,132,136,139-140,145-146,149,153-154,159,169
Hell 45,65,126
Herod 51,55
Hermeneuo 160
Hermeneutics 107-108,160,162-163,170

Historical 80,101,106-108,128,162-163
Holiness 24,38,58,72,74,123,154
Holy Spirit 9,44-45,51,53-62,79,85,95,97
103-107,109,123,132
Hosea 89
Hosts 28,52,146
Host of Heaven 145
Human Government 166-167
Humanist 139,142

I

I AM 20-22,30,36,38-39,42,46-48,51-52,75,125
Illumination 80,103-106,111
Immensity 28-29,32,45
Immutable 41,43,114,162
Incarnation 23,50,84,92,168
Indwelling 58,60,62,105
Inerrant 58,80,92-94
Infallible 93
Infinite 27,40-42
Inheritance 9,41,61,122,147,154-155
Inorganic 135-136,138-141
Inscripturation 79-80,92,94-95,110
Institute for Creation Research 134,137
Inspiration 79-80,86-87,93,95-99,101-102
Invisible 83,145-147,155,159
Intellect 54-55,90,140,142
International Counsel on Biblical Inerrancy 93
Interpretation 79-80,85,106-108,157,159-160,162-164
Intuition 81,83
Ireland 113
Isaiah 89-91
Israel 12,14-15,17,20,29-30,35,46-47,52,90,98
104,106,108,117-119,121,123,130,147,160,163-164,167-168

J

Jacob 88-90,123,167
Jehovah 20,44,47,151
Jerusalem 14,16-17,89,91,104,117-118,123,149,153
Jews 14,20-21,29,47-48,59,66,68,70,94
102,109,122
Job 130,166
John the Baptist 71,151,154
Jonah 103-104
Judaism 82,94
Judah 10,11
Judges 119,198
Judgment 31,54-55,82,85,105,119,121-122
164-165,168
Judgment Seat 121
Judicial 106
Justification 72,75,129,152

K

King James 110,158
King of Israel 14,52,130,147
King of Kings 120

L

Latin 115
Lake of Fire 120,123-124,169
Law 24,30,35,69,74-75,85-86,89,98,103,108
117,126,129,135,154,166,168
Legion 145-146
Levado 29
Literal 80,106-107,114,158,160,162-164
Lord of Lords 120
Lord's Supper 163
Lot 89
Love 27,35-36,44,46,71,75,82,89
Lucius 51,55
Luke 28,152

Lysander 69
Lystra 84

M

Macedonia 75-76,89
Macedonian Jailer 76
Magog 169
Manaen 51,55
Manuscripts 94,109
Marriage 121,150
Marriage Supper 121
Matter 135-138
Mediator 52
Mercy 13,66,72,76
Mercy Seat 154
Messengers 15,145,151-152,154
Messiah 11-19,22,24,49,118,123,168
Micah 89
Michael 154
Midian 20,30,46
Midtribulational 114
Might 22,49,120,148,154
Mighty God 22,49
Millennial Kingdom 121-123,160,169
Millennium 123-124,158,160
Ministering Spirits 147,154
Missionary 75,143,161
Mobile 41
Modalism 162
Moses 20,30,46-47,71,90-91,98,103,168
Mount Sinai 167
Mystery 71,117,158
Mysticism 94,107

N

Natural 81-83,86,89,106,126,168,162
Naturalistic 126,134,137

Naturalistic Evolution 134
Nature 27,34,39,41,56,62,83-84,88,90,94,104
114,126,128-131,133
Nature of Man 126,128
Nazareth 22,48
Nebuchadnezzar 91
New Hebrides 143
Nicodemus 130-131
Niger 51,55
Noah 166-167

O

Onanokees 133
Omega 39
Omnipotence 38
Omnipresence 32
Omniscience 39
Organic 135-141
Origin 89,93,133-134,136-138
Original Sin 125

P

Passe Graphe 96-97
Passover 168
Patmos 148
Paul 24-25,55-56,58-62,68-71,73,75-76,78,82,84
89-90,95,98,106,127,148,154,161,163,165,168
Pentecost 104,161,163
Person 12,29,44-45,51-52,54,57-58,60-62,81,86,103
Peter 9,38,51,57-58,85,88-89,104,148,152
Pharisee 40
Philippi 25,104
Philosophy 126
Piltdown Man 138
Plenary 79,93,97
Pneumatology 53
Pontius Pilate 125

Postmillennial 114,160
Posttribulational 114,160
Power 16,22,28,38-39,44,49,55,58,62-63,66-67
69-70,76,78,83,85-86,90,100-102,104,140,145,148,154,170
Preincarnate 92,151
Premillennial 114,160
Pretribulational 114,161
Preservation 79-80,94,97,102,109-111,145
Prince 22,49,118
Principalities 28,145,154
Progressive Creationism 142
Progressive Dispensationalism 161
Progressive Revelation 161
Promise 12,43,59,61,116,119,167-168
Prophecy 14,19,85,114,118,149
Prophet 21,30,47,51,55,74-75,84,87,103
118,120,124,168
Prophetic 71,85,89,102-103,114
Propitiation 72
Proselyte 168
Protestant 102
Psychiatrists 126
Psychology 88,126,128-129

R

Rationalism 107
Reason 10,25,30,62,78,82-83,100,107
114,121,128,141-142,158
Rahab 152
Rapture 115-117,119,160-161
Redeemer 12,52
Redeemed 124
Redemption 56,61,71-72,75
Resurrection 23,30-31,49
Revelation 14,38-39,79-81,83-87,89,92,94-95
97-98,103,106-107,110,117,122,124,148-149,152,159-161,165
168-169

Righteousness...........................24,34,37,50,54-55,66,72-75,83
87,92,96,99,105,116,118-119,123,167,169
Roman Empire... 160
Rome 68

S

Sacrifice...84,98,118-119,166
Saints......................... 10,56,58,88,91-92,103-104,114-116,122
152,155,169
Salvation..........................16,61,65-68,70-73,76,78,83,85,106
126,147,154,157,159-160,163-164
Sanctification.. 72
Satan.................................. 23,44,49,51,57,86,106,124,165,169
Satanic Blindness 106
Sapphira... 51,57
Sarai.. 151
Saul...13,51,55-56
Savior 10,12,17,30,104,165
Science 45,94,108,134-140,160
Sealing... 58,61
Seals 119
Second Advent 121,123
Second Blessing 58
Second Coming 121-122
Senses 81,144
Septuagint 103,110
Seraphim... 89,154
Serpent... 127
Seventy-weeks.. 118
Shema 29
Silas 75-76,84
Simeon.. 51,55
Simon 104
Sin................. 13,16,24-25,38,54-85,60,65,68,70-73,75,78,82,98
101-102,105,117-118,125-130,132,165-169

Son 14,22,24,30-31,37,44-49,67,75,84,87
104,116,122-123,146
Soteriology 65
Sovereign 41,65,68,170
Spain 113
Spirit 9,15,28-29,32-33,41,43-45,51,53-63
68,72,79,82-83,85,90,95-97,100,103-109,123,129,131-132,140
145-147,149,152-155
Spirit Stuff 28,147
Spiritual Blindness 105
Steward 122,161,164,166-169
Stewardship 159,161
Sunday Express 116
Sword 76,100,120,144

T

Temple 14,20-22,47-48,60,89,91,117
Ten Commandments 91
Textual Criticism 109
Theistic Evolution 142
Theology Proper 27
Theopneustos 96
Thomas 23,36,49-50
Throne 13-14,24,32,50,122-123,145,149,154
Timothy 78
Tokoa 147
Tongues 18,58,71,73,167
Total Depravity 128
Tower of Babel 167
Tradition 81-83,103
Translation 79,81,103,110,115,158
Tribulation 116,118-122,160
Trinity 44-45,104
Trumpets 115,117,119
Truth 9-10,22,36-37,41,44,49,52,54-56,60-61,66
68-69,73,78,80-84,86-87,89,91-93,95,100,102-106,110,116
123,125,134,136-137,139,161-162,170

Twin 23,49,117

U
Ultradispensationalism 161,163
Unity 29,159,162
Universe 158,160,197

V
Verbal 79,90-91,93,97
Verbal Inspiration 79,97
Virgin 12,14
Visible 145-146

W
Watchtower Bible & Tract 44-45
Will 41,54-56,62
Writings 56,79,96,103

Y
YHWH 20,29,47,115

Z
Zion 16,149,153

Person Index

B

Bernal, J.D., ... 138
Boice, James M., ... 93
Bryan, William Jennings 142
Brooks, Keith l., ... 146
Bullinger, E.W., ... 126

C

Castro 128
Chambers, Oswald 126
Colson, Charles 159
Constantine 160
Cooper, David L., ... 107

D

Draper, Edythe 71, 142, 159

E
Enns, Paul 81,84,96,101,160-161
Easton, M.G. 159

F
Feder, Don 128
Franco 131

G
Geisler, Norman L., ... 102
Gish, Duane T., ... 137
Gower, Ralph 108
Goolde, George 94

H
Hare, George 87,158,166-167
Hitler 113,128
Hugo, Victor 141

L
Lennon 128
Lewis, C.S. 11,73,132

M
MacArthur, John 101
McGee, J. Vernon 136-137
Mora 138
Morgan, G. Campbell 132
Mussolini 128

N
Naylor, R.H. 113
Newton, Isaac 134-135,140
Nilsson, Heribert 139
Nix, William E., ... 102

O

Orr, James 90,158

P

Paton, John G., ... 143-144
Pavlic, James 162
Payson 65
Pentz, Croft M., ... 133
Peretti, Frank 134

R

Russell, Charles Taze 107
Ryrie, Charles C., ... 92-93,97,157

S

Scofield, C.H. 162
Shannon, Robert C., ... 113
Shinn, Garland, ... 28-29,34,42,45
Smith, Joseph 107
Spurgeon, Charles H., ... 65,69
Stuart, Charles M., ... 88
Vardiman, Larry 134-135

W

Walker, W.L. 158
Warfield, Benjamin B., ... 96
Wheeler, R.L., ... 71

Y

Young, E.J., ... 93-94,97

www.ingramcontent.com/pod-product-compliance
Lightning Source LLC
Chambersburg PA
CBHW062038220426
43662CB00010B/1555